Everyday & Sunday

When Guy Watson began growing vegetables organically on his family's farm in South Devon, it was the beginning of Riverford Organic. They are now one of the country's largest independent organic growers and pioneering veg box suppliers, regularly garnering critical acclaim for their delivery service and Field Kitchen restaurant. Riverford's awards include the Soil Association's Best Organic Retailer 2009, the *Observer* Ethical Awards' Best Business 2009 and Best Online Retailer 2010, and the *Observer Food Monthly*'s Best Ethical Restaurant 2009 and 2010.

Month by month, *Everyday & Sunday* describes what vegetables are in season and the best ways to use them, with recipes for quick, everyday meals alongside one or two for a more celebratory dish, or an indulgent Sunday feast. From a warming kale gratin in March, to a fresh salad of braised Little Gems and mint in June or a Swiss chard, squash and blue cheese torte in October, Jane Baxter's simple and inspiring recipes will help you to make the best of your veg, all year round.

Guy Watson began farming organically in 1985, with a wheel-barrow and a borrowed tractor, on three acres of the Watson family farm in South Devon. Delivering his vegetables to local shops soon morphed into a ground-breaking home delivery box scheme that has sister farms nationwide growing and packing vegetables for customers locally. Riverford has become one of the country's largest independent organic growers certified by the Soil Association.

Jane Baxter has been head chef at Riverford's award-winning farm restaurant, the Field Kitchen, since 2005. Jane trained in Dartmouth at the Carved Angel with Joyce Molyneux, before moving on to the River Café in London. Subsequent years of travelling and cooking her way around the southern hemisphere and visits to the Puglia region of Italy have greatly influenced her cooking style.

Guy Watson & Jane Baxter

Everyday & Sunday recipes from

Riverford Farm

FOURTH ESTATE • *London*

First published in Great Britain by
Fourth Estate
a division of HarperCollins*Publishers*
77–85 Fulham Palace Road
London W6 8JB
www.4thestate.co.uk

9 8 7 6 5 4 3 2 1

A catalogue record for this book is
available from the British Library

ISBN 978-0-00-738826-4

Typeset by Birdy Book Design
Printed and bound by Butler Tanner and Dennis Ltd, Frome

Contents

Acknowledgements

A massive thank you to Samantha Miller, who has worked tirelessly to make the Field Kitchen what it is. She is a great friend, colleague and a constant support to the team. And to all the staff at the Field Kitchen (past and present) who have worked so hard with commitment, enthusiasm and great humour. In particular: Ben Bulger, Ben Edwards, Georgie Sawry-Cookson, Robin, Jenny, Carrie, Kate Dahill, Addz, Auntie Pauline, Darran, Mother Vanessa, Super Rita, Jenna, Katie B, Richard, Tara, Heath, Sharman, Sarah, Russell, Fluffy Lizzie, Popey, Conrad and all the rest. A big thank you to all at Fourth Estate, in particular Louise Haines, Julian Humphries, Ed Park and Georgia Mason, and to everyone who has donated recipes to the book.

Jane Baxter

Managing cooks and farmers is harder than herding a yardful of cats. The task of coordinating and pulling this book together fell to Kirsty Hale, who has performed it with unerring enthusiasm, grace, determination and good judgement.

Growing vegetables and running a box scheme involves occasional inspiration but more often meticulous planning, careful accumulation of experience and a lot of hard work. That work is often done under conditions that, in the 21st century, the huge majority would find intolerable. Pulling leeks in the driving rain in January with ten pounds of mud on each foot requires a resilience possessed by very few. Keeping 40,000 boxes full, balanced and interesting, week in week out, whatever the elements throw at us is what my 400 staff are good at, allowing me the time to write books, open restaurants and dream up the next crazy project.

One of these projects is the 'Riverford Cooks': a loose affiliation of like-minded, ingredients-inspired cooks who would get close and intimate in homes, in the classroom, at shows, in a yurt – anywhere people could come together to learn about and share food. You can only go so far with a book; smelling, tasting and sharing is always going to have a more lasting influence. Some of those cooks have contributed to this book and a few are detailed on page 348.

Kirsty wanted to thank all the staff here at the farm who tried out recipes from the book: Mark, Jennie, Sarah, Laura R, Laura C, Gail, Martine, Catherine, Peter, Polly, Liam, Tressa, Mel, Lillie, David, Rob, Gemma, Kelly and Tom.

Lastly, I would like to thank our customers for their support and trust in Riverford, which has allowed us to farm and trade with an eye to the long term in a way that seems right to us rather than chasing every trend in a fickle market. In particular, I would like to thank those who have recommended us to their friends. We have always been better at growing veg than selling it; without your help much of it would have been wasted in the fields.

Guy Watson

Why another cook book?

When, after years of exponential growth, sales of our vegetable boxes quite suddenly plateaued in early 2007, it took a while to figure out why. Customers, and even ex-customers, still seemed to like us and our vegetables but, when asked in a customer survey how easy life is with a veg box only 5 per cent replied 'really easy.' Almost two-thirds found it 'fairly easy' (read 'a bit difficult'), while a full third found it 'a struggle'. A struggle might be relished when doing a crossword or climbing Ben Nevis, but these are matters of choice. Feeding the family is obligatory; it's part of our busy, routine, everyday lives and we want it to be straightforward. Sixty years of steadily growing advertising budgets have incessantly pushed processed food as a convenient alternative, insidiously suggesting that only a Neanderthal or a fool would peel a potato or pod a bean. Thankfully, some held out, working away in isolated kitchens cooking what was then deeply unfashionable: food made from scratch, using local and seasonal ingredients. Their rebellion is spreading, and has even become fashionable. Many now aspire to cook seasonal food from scratch but, after two generations of passive surrender to the food industry, few have the confidence and skill to make it easy.

Despite the hype from celebrity chefs with their endless fantasy cookery programmes and professed enthusiasm for seasonality, despite the best endeavours of our government with its 'five-a-day' campaign, the consumption of fresh, unprocessed vegetables continues to decline (a 45 per cent decline in consumption of fresh green vegetables over thirty years, with a continuing 20 per cent decline in the last ten years). Riverford's future, the future of the farmers who supply us and, to some extent, the nation's health depend on reversing this 60-year trend. Nagging and guilt does not work, even if backed up by statistics and health warnings. If it is going to happen every day, we have to make cooking with seasonal, fresh ingredients easy for the 95 per cent who find it a struggle. That is the purpose of this book.

The kitchen challenge
The challenge lies not at the table – there is no self-denial here – but in the kitchen, with the confidence and skills of the cook. Jane's cooking in our Field Kitchen restaurant and the recipes in our first Riverford cook book have shown that eating locally and seasonally is highly enjoyable. While those recipes were practical and determinedly 'non-poncy' (Jane's term), feedback from readers and customers showed that the work in the kitchen could be simpler, and the recipes remain inspiring and unusual. The 'everyday' recipes in this book are

there to broaden everyone's culinary repertoire, and some of them – I hope – will become the kind of favourites you resort to whenever you are under pressure to feed the household without the time to think too hard about it. That will be one measure of our success: I would love to think that there might be a few households where radicchio pasta in the late autumn or courgette fritters in the summer might be as unremarkable as a seasonless spag bol. We've also included a few more challenging dishes from the Riverford Field Kitchen, something for the weekend or more celebratory occasions – that's the 'Sunday' bit in the title. Some of these Sunday dishes can also be used on their own as part of your everyday cooking as well as part of a more lavish meal.

In 2008, with sales on the slide, I employed a managing director to instil some order in my chaotic business and set off on a cooking odyssey in the hope of understanding why my freakishly high vegetable consumption was not the norm. Our box scheme has always been a personal affair, built on the assumption that most of our customers were like me and would therefore enjoy cooking similar meals with similar ingredients. My odyssey started by inviting myself into the homes of thirty customers and ex-customers to cook with them and share the meal with them and their friends. Cooking in their clean kitchens soon made me realise that our insistence on delivering the veg complete with a good part of the field it had grown in was ridiculous. More than one said they organised their cleaning around the arrival of the box. We now brush the roots and are reluctantly (because it reduces shelf-life) but pragmatically moving towards washing the worst offenders.

Cooking with cabbages
A more significant and harder problem to solve is that even if our customers are often good and experienced cooks, they are seldom used to making the most of seasonal veg in a country where cabbages are in season all year but unheated tomatoes are in season for ten weeks, peppers for six and aubergines for about four. For the last two generations, the cooking that has taken place in the nation's kitchens has increasingly focused on the exotic, to the extent that today's generation are more confident with peppers and lemongrass than they are with cabbage and parsley. We do now have growers in Italy and Spain and import aubergines, tomatoes, and peppers (I am not a diehard localist) but if we are to survive without straying uncomfortably far from our founding principles, we need to give our customers more confidence with traditional vegetables like cabbage, rhubarb and swede, a few new ideas for cauliflowers and chard, and help them to appreciate the potential of the less conventional celeriac, romanesco, kohlrabi and artichokes.

The Riverford Cooks

Perhaps I should not be writing this at all because, as an impatient mild dyslexic who needs glasses but can never find them, I seldom open a recipe book. I'm not great in social situations either, but I had my best New Year ever cooking a huge paella for the first time with three friends. I like to get to know people, and to learn new recipes and cooking techniques by cooking with them. This is how the cooking odyssey has developed: a group of people cooking together under the loose guidance of one of our fifty (and growing) Riverford Cooks. Some of these cooks are well-trained and experienced professionals, some of them talented and enthusiastic amateurs with a gift for inspiring others. They have a wide range of styles but are united in an enthusiasm for working with the best fresh, seasonal ingredients. We have cooked at festivals, in the woods, in shops, cafés and shopping centres, in a yurt in an orchard and on a London city farm, in people's homes, in my bus in a field of artichokes, on the beach – anywhere we can get a group of people together around a gas burner and chopping board at minimal expense. Participants have included customers, potential customers and staff. This is the best staff training we have ever done: it brings people together, makes them more authoritative about what Riverford does, gets us all thinking about flavour and quality and, most importantly of all, is fun. Some of the recipes included here are from those Riverford Cooks and we have introduced those who have contributed at the end of the book.

Cooking and eating habits are deeply ingrained in our behaviour, usually having been established at an early age through example and repetition. Like many aspects of our culture, they are hard to change for the better, easily eroded for the worse and hard to reclaim once lost. Now that people are more likely to have their views on food shaped by TV chefs than be taught to cook by their parents, we need some help. I am hoping that this book and our group of Riverford Cooks will give people practical help to develop their confidence and skills, making the everyday cooking of seasonal vegetables an easy and enjoyable part of life. If you would like to join our cooking odyssey as a Riverford Cook, by hosting an event, providing a venue or just participating, you can find more information on our website: www.riverford. co.uk

Reversing the trend

Reversing a half-century trend, in opposition to a well-funded processed food industry, will not be easy and will not happen fast but the kitchen-led rebellion is gathering some pace. Aspirations are turning into action and we will continue to do what we can to support that conversion. After three and a half difficult years, our sales are showing some signs of growth. We even have the occasional customer asking for more cabbage.

Guy Watson, 2011

Jane's store cupboard

If I wasn't a parent my fridge would probably be quite bare, with a bit of mouldy cheese and a can of Stella, the chef's essential! However, nowadays, apart from yoghurts and juice, I normally have the makings of a quick stir-fry to go with rice or couscous for my son, David. When you're coming home from work at six, to a hungry child, food has to arrive almost immediately. I have also become quite a dab hand at the two-pan roast dinner (refrying par-boiled potatoes in one and doing chicken, green veg and gravy in another). My mum's tip for great gravy is Compton's Gravy Salts which, along with concentrated chicken stock, guarantee a good result.

To help you cook from this book I have put together a few store cupboard essentials – nothing too taxing to source, but ingredients that are good to have around and will help to create an interesting but simple meal from your vegetables.

Herbs and spices
The longer dried herbs and spices hang around for, the more flavour they lose, so it is always best to use as fresh as possible. Generally, it is preferable to use fresh herbs but the dried ones have their place. I would definitely stock dried oregano, thyme, bay and mint.

The following spices are used throughout this book:
Cumin, coriander, cardamom, caraway, fennel seeds, cayenne, nutmeg, cinnamon, ginger, mustard seeds, turmeric, paprika – smoked and sweet, and dried whole chillies.

To achieve maximum flavour, it is best to dry-roast whole spices before grinding.

Saffron is also a basic to me but might seem extravagant to others – use it sparingly.

Italian
Capers, olives and anchovies: salted capers and anchovies are the best quality but can be quite hard to find. If you are using capers in brine or vinegar be sure to soak them well before using.

Oils
Good-quality extra virgin olive oil, a basic olive oil, sunflower or rapeseed oil, walnut and sesame oil.

Always cook with your basic olive oil and save the more expensive, fuller flavoured oil for dressings and drizzling over vegetables. Giancarlo Ceci's oils that are stocked by Riverford are good quality and value.

Vinegars
Balsamic, red and white wine vinegar and rice vinegar.

In addition to the standard vinegars, the rice vinegar makes an interesting store cupboard basic and is good for dressing vegetables in Asian-inspired salads.

Grains, pulses and pastas
Risotto and basmati rice, couscous, puy lentils, haricot or cannellini beans, chickpeas and pasta.

Be sure to buy good-quality arborio rice to use in making risottos. As with pasta, it can be turned into a substantial meal – most vegetables can be added to a risotto or turned into a pasta sauce. Beans and lentils are a staple in the Field Kitchen and are incorporated into a huge number of our meat and vegetable dishes.

Asian
Tamarind paste, fish sauce, creamed coconut, coconut milk, soy sauce and kecap manis.

There are quite a few Asian-inspired dishes in this book so the above are a bonus to have around. Tamarind paste is easier to use than the tamarind pod that has to be soaked. Kecap manis is a thick sweetened Malaysian soy available in Asian supermarkets or online. It's worth using in stir fries and experimenting with.

Flours
Plain, self-raising, gram and rice flour.

Apart from the obvious flours, we tend to use gram and rice flour frequently in the Field Kitchen. Gram flour is made from chickpeas and is also known as besan. It imparts a nutty flavour and is widely used, for example in the batter of onion bhajis. We use gram and rice flour in batters and cakes, as they are gluten free and give an interesting texture and flavour.

Nuts
Ground and flaked almonds, pine nuts, walnuts, pistachios and pecans.

Incorporating a small quantity of nuts into a dressing before tossing through your roasted or steamed veg can really lift a dish. Don't have them hanging around for too long though and always keep them in a sealed container. Toasting before using strengthens the flavour.

Basics
Other basic ingredients that are always useful: mustard (wholegrain, Dijon and English), honey, tomato purée, tinned tomatoes (it is worth investing in a good-quality organic brand – What on Earth are good), tahini, caster and soft brown sugar.

Stock
Good stock is essential to add flavour in a dish. There are readily available pre-prepared stocks and some good bouillon powders, but it's sometimes best to make your own. To use up the odds and ends in your veg box, make a vegetable stock.

Vegetable stock
Chop up the woody outer stalks of celery, the odd carrot, and other vegetable scraps (but not starchy vegetables such as potatoes and parsnips).

Put the vegetables in a large pan and cover with water. Add a few herbs (such as bay leaves, thyme sprigs or parsley stalks) if you have them.

Simmer for about 30 minutes. Strain.

Stock will keep for a few days in the fridge, or can be frozen in batches for later use. If you're not vegetarian, try making a chicken stock; chicken carcasses can be ordered from Riverford alongside a meat box, or try your local butcher.

Chicken Stock
1 chicken carcass
½ onion
1 celery stick – use tough outside ones
½ leek or the top of 1 leek
1 bay leaf
5 peppercorns
1 bunch of parsley stalks
sprig of thyme
giblets from chicken, excluding the liver

Chop up the chicken bones and roast in a medium oven for 30–45 minutes until browned.

Transfer to a stockpot. Deglaze the roasting pan with a little hot water and scrape off the 'gubbins' into the pot.

Roughly chop the vegetables, add to the pot and just cover with water. Add the rest of the ingredients. Bring up to the boil and simmer gently for 3–4 hours, then strain. The stock can then be refrigerated when cool, this makes it easy to remove fat from the top, or it can be reduced for a stronger flavour.

Specialist ingredients

Two slightly out of the ordinary ingredients that appear on a few occasions in recipes are corn tortillas and salt cod. I think chefs do become obsessive about the odd thing. There was definitely a smoked paprika outbreak in the mid-nineties.

There is an easily available brand of corn tortillas in most good food shops but for superior freshly made ones, go to the website of the Cool Chile Company with their new mega tortilla press apparently called El Monstruo.

Salt cod can be bought in various forms from Caribbean shops, in small packs from some fishmongers and from online retailers.

Storage tips

Keep it fresh
Freshness is a major determinant of the flavour – and nutritional value – of vegetables. We grow, pick, pack and deliver ourselves, so our vegetables are as fresh as they can be when they reach the doorstep. They then need to be treated right until you get to eat them. Centrally heated houses do most vegetables no favours and their shelf life can halve for every 10°C rise in temperature. Here are a few useful storage ideas to keep your vegetables in the best condition possible.

Some general tips when unpacking your veg box
Keep everything cool and give priority in the fridge to leafy salads, greens and broccoli.

A good place to store vegetables is in a cupboard or larder on a north-facing wall. It should have an airbrick to allow air to circulate. Otherwise, it can work well to hang a vegetable rack outside on a shaded wall. You could also try a Riverford ecosafe: a wooden cupboard large enough to store a veg box, which you surround with soil and compost to keep it cool (see picture on page xx). It also has a planter on top for herbs or flowers. If you've got room, a vegetable rack in a cool room or dry outhouse is a good idea for root vegetables and cabbages, and you can even use a car boot in the winter (particularly useful for excess vegetables around Christmas time).

We do put some of our vegetables in plastic bags; they are all recyclable and can help retain the moisture of some vegetables in the fridge, for example leafy greens, spinach, chard, green beans, rhubarb and wild garlic.

Potatoes
Keep them cool and in the dark to stop them sprouting. Riverford's come ready to store in a paper bag. After Christmas, when they're keen to start sprouting, keep them in the fridge to slow down this urge. Never keep potatoes in plastic – they'll sweat and turn mouldy.

Beetroots, carrots, turnips, kohlrabi and fennel
Keep the moisture in the vegetable and not the leaves by removing any leafy tops as soon as possible.

Tomatoes
Tomatoes don't like being kept below 10°C, so are best kept at room temperature or, in summer, in a cool vegetable rack, rather than the fridge.

Broad beans
It's best to leave broad beans in their pods until needed for cooking.

Sweetcorn
We deliver sweetcorn in its husk – the perfect storage container. Keep in the fridge, just as they are.

Garlic
Keep the wet and wild varieties in the fridge, but dry garlic will be happy in a vegetable rack or cool store.

Herbs and chillies
It's best to eat these as fresh as possible. Some can be hung and dried, such as chillies, thyme and rosemary, and others can be frozen and crumbled in cooking, for example basil and tarragon.

Leeks
The bottom of the fridge or a cool vegetable rack is fine for leeks.

Onions
Keep salad and spring onions in the fridge. Brown or red dried onions should be kept cool and dry, a vegetable rack or hanging net bag is ideal.

Squash
Keep squash and pumpkins in the warm and dry – on a kitchen shelf for example. Some squash will last all winter, but pumpkins won't keep for long.

Radishes
You can revive limp radishes by putting them in a cup of cold water. They will absorb the moisture and firm up again.

We have lots of useful vegetable storage, preparation and simple cooking tips available on our website, many in short video clips. From preparing artichokes to braising beetroot tops, find more help at www.riverford.co.uk/cook

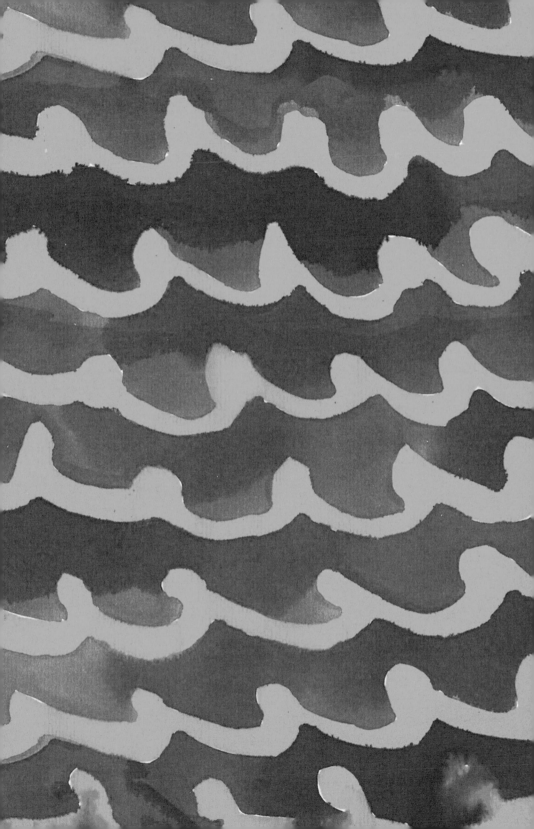

Everyday

Celeriac and Potato Mash
Anna's Jerusalem Artichoke Soup with Prawns and Paprika
Quick Fried Grated Celeriac
Sausage Stew with Celeriac and Kale
Beef in Newcastle Brown Ale with Horseradish Dumplings
Francesca's Roast Vegetables with Lime Pickle
Tartine Gratinée à l'Oignon
Mashed Roots
Seville Orange Marmalade
Parsnip and Walnut Beignets
Red Onion Confit

Sunday

Warm Pheasant Salad with Pomegranate and Walnuts
Kale and Potato Cakes
Braised Red Cabbage with Beetroot and Orange
Lemon and Orange Tart

JANUARY

Eat stew and be happy

The days are short; the sun, when we see it, is low; the soil is finally cold and dormant and nothing is growing as we wait for a new season to begin. On the coastal fringes, any mild spells bring on occasional flushes of cauliflower and perhaps the first purple sprouting broccoli but, for greens, we are mainly dependent on what grew before Christmas and is hardy enough to withstand the frost and battering of winter gales. Savoy and January King cabbages and the kales all seem to benefit from slower growth and are at their best after some hard winter weather. Of the kales, Jane favours the regal-looking blistered leaves of cavolo nero (or black kale, as we called it for years before it became trendy courtesy of the River Café). Cavolo nero can succumb to really hard frost, however, leaving only the more traditional, lighter green and easier-to-grow curly kale found pre-chopped in most supermarkets. Curly kale can be almost as good as cavolo nero once it has had plenty of frost but is best avoided in the autumn.

Leeks are a stalwart as long as the ground is not frozen hard enough to stop us pulling them. You will find that, as the winter progresses, leeks get shorter and stouter, normally with darker leaves. We move from the upright, high-yielding but tender autumn varieties into the slower-growing, more flavoursome, robust and traditionally squat varieties such as Musselburgh that see us through to the end of the season in April.

From the barn

From our stores we are grateful for a good supply of potatoes, carrots, the better-keeping varieties of winter squash, onions, beetroot and celeriac. The slow-growing celeriac takes a full season to develop its ugly, wrinkled but fine-tasting roots (OK, technically it's a hypocotyl, for the botanists among you), which we bring in to store in November. The flavour is similar to celery (less water, less crunch but a deeper flavour with a touch of smokiness), with more to offer the cook: simply mashed with potato, quick-fried, in stews, in stocks (use the peelings, allowing any grit to settle out), in soups (wonderful, especially with truffle oil), in gratins, or in salads (such as the classic staple of northern Europe, celeriac rémoulade). Celeriac has the added benefit that it can be stored for weeks in the fridge; in our cold stores we're able to keep them right through to the spring.

Hardy roots

When we get a few consecutive dry days, allowing the soil in the better drained fields to dry enough for harvesting machinery to work, there is a scurry of activity as we grab a few loads of parsnips and Jerusalem artichokes. Unlike the stored crops that survive the winter happily in a barn, neither parsnips nor root artichokes store well out of the soil so must be harvested relatively frequently and sold fresh. Parsnips are at their best in January – they have had enough cold to develop their full sweetness but are still fully dormant. Later in the season, as temperatures and day length increase, their cores will become woody as they prepare to re-grow and throw a seed head. We deliver our roots unwashed on the basis that washing always damages the skin and causes them to deteriorate much more quickly; this is particularly the case for parsnips. With the help of a good vegetable brush, provided you soak them for a few minutes first, washing is very quick and your roots will taste much better than those that have had their skins scuffed in the factory-washing process, removing their natural barrier to decay.

Root artichokes with their knobbly, ginger-like shape are also at their best. Their legendary (and fully justified) reputation of inducing flatulence makes them a contentious item in our vegetable boxes, but they are wonderful in a simple soup, perhaps with the addition of toasted and crushed hazelnuts, or see Anna's Jerusalem Artichoke Soup with Prawns and Paprika on page 10. Some say that drinking fennel tea reduces their potency.

Oranges at their best

Most citrus are in season in the northern hemisphere from November to April (lemons run for longer, from October to June) and are at their peak in January; they are in a different league to the South African and South American fruit we see during the summer. Most of the lemons, oranges, grapefruit and clementines we sell come from a group of small organic growers in the hills behind Almería in southern Spain, who consistently grow fabulously sweet, juicy and relatively easily peeled fruit. They reckon it is down to the soil. I suspect it has as much to do with getting it from the tree to the mouth quickly without any wholesalers holding stock in between – citrus will maintain its appearance for weeks in cold store but it loses any ability to excite the palate.

Sevilles normally arrive in mid-January for the annual marmalade fest. Get on with it, by February they are coming out of store and are past their best. We deliver blood oranges in January and February, working with a grower in

Sicily. Jane's Lemon and Orange Tart (page 25) has a particularly good colour and flavour when made with these; they're a vibrant addition to a salad too.

All but the most dilettante, lightweight vegetable eaters and box customers are happy with a few weeks of no-nonsense English winter veg; they are essential ingredients in the warming soups and stews that are so appealing at this time of year. I urge you to embrace winter, turn your back on vain grabs at distant exotica, make some marmalade and enjoy your local roots and greens at their robust winter best.

Quick and easy ideas
JERUSALEM ARTICHOKES

Jerusalem artichoke mash

Mash cooked Jerusalem artichokes and potatoes together (a drizzle of truffle oil makes a lovely addition).

Jerusalem artichoke fritters

Peel and grate Jerusalem artichokes, add a grated onion and squeeze out excess moisture. Bind together with an egg and sifted flour to dropping consistency. Season. Cook in batches in oil and butter in a shallow frying pan. Use a dessertspoon of the mixture for each pancake, squashing them down with the back of the spoon and frying until golden brown on both sides.

Jerusalem artichoke crisps

Peel and finely slice Jerusalem artichokes. Dry well and deep-fry until golden. Sprinkle with salt and smoked paprika.

Fresh artichoke salad

Peel and thinly slice Jerusalem artichokes, mix with salad dressing or the mustard dressing on page 71, cover and leave to marinate in the fridge overnight. Serve as a salad or as an accompaniment to cold meats.

Sizzled artichokes

Cook bacon lardons in a shallow frying pan until the fat is released and the bacon crispy. Remove the bacon from the pan. Add peeled, chopped Jerusalem artichokes and shredded sage leaves, mix well, cover and cook for 10–15 minutes or until tender. Return the bacon to the pan, season and sprinkle with a little balsamic vinegar. A great partner for grilled scallops.

EVERYDAY

Celeriac and Potato Mash

The key to this dish is cooking the celeriac in milk, with the garlic. The garlic is sweeter once it's cooked and, when it is creamed with the celeriac, tastes fantastic. The addition of the slightly reduced milk gives even more flavour to the final mash. You can use a potato masher, but you'll get smoother fluffier results if you can use a food mill (mouli légumes). It can be served with a huge range of dishes, but is particularly good with any stew with a rich gravy.

Serves 4–6

1 celeriac, peeled and cut into 1–2cm chunks
6 garlic cloves, peeled
milk
sea salt and freshly ground black pepper
2 baking or large potatoes, peeled and cut into 2cm chunks
1 teaspoon Dijon mustard
30g unsalted butter, melted
cream (optional)

Place the celeriac in a pan with the garlic and just enough milk to cover. Season, bring to a boil and simmer for about 20 minutes until tender.

Boil the potatoes separately in salted water until tender. Drain.

When both are ready, arrange a food mill over a pan containing the mustard and butter. Remove the celeriac and garlic from the milk with a slotted spoon and place them into the mouli with the drained potatoes. Pass the vegetables through the mill and beat with a wooden spoon. Season well and, if the mash is too stiff, add a little of the celeriac cooking milk or some cream to let it down.

Anna's Jerusalem Artichoke Soup with Prawns and Paprika

This is a recipe from one of our Riverford Cooks, Anna Colquhoun. It can work as a basic artichoke soup recipe, but the addition of the prawns and paprika make it a special and more unusual dish. You can get away without peeling Jerusalem artichokes if you scrub them really well, but you will need to use a sieve or food mill to get the final soup smooth. If you do peel them, use a short sharp knife instead of a peeler – it's easier to negotiate the knobbly bits. You might have to slice off some of the more difficult lumps but you'll only lose a small amount of flesh, so don't worry about it.

Serves 4–6

1 small onion, finely chopped
2 tablespoons olive oil
sea salt and finely ground black pepper
500g Jerusalem artichokes, peeled and roughly chopped
1 sprig of thyme
1 bay leaf
pinch of grated nutmeg
12 large raw prawns, peeled and deveined
1 teaspoon smoked paprika
1 teaspoon sweet paprika
2 tablespoons good-quality extra virgin olive oil
handful of chives, snipped, to serve (optional)

In a heavy-based saucepan, cook the onion gently in half the olive oil with a pinch of salt over a low heat until soft but not coloured; it will take 10–15 minutes. Add the artichokes, thyme and bay, cover and cook gently for a further 10 minutes. Add enough water to barely cover the artichokes. Bring to a boil and simmer for another 15 minutes, or until the artichokes are tender. Remove the herbs and blend the soup until smooth in a blender or food processor, or with a stick blender, adding extra water if required until the consistency is as you prefer. Check the seasoning and add a little grated nutmeg. Keep warm.

Heat the remaining olive oil in a frying pan. Season the prawns with salt and pepper, nutmeg and a little of the sweet and smoked paprika and fry quickly on both sides.

Combine the rest of the paprika with the extra virgin olive oil.

Serve the soup in warmed bowls, each topped with 2 or 3 prawns, a drizzle of the paprika oil and a sprinkle of chives, if you have some.

Quick Fried Grated Celeriac

This is a great side dish to serve with duck, sausages or pork. To prepare celeriac, chop off the top and all the roots, then use a short sharp serrated knife (a tomato knife is ideal) to saw off the skin around the edges. Don't bother with a vegetable peeler, and don't worry if you waste a bit of flesh. If chives or parsley aren't available, use rosemary or sage instead. Some chopped, toasted hazelnuts to finish the dish would be good.

Serves 4

1 celeriac
25g unsalted butter
1 tablespoon olive oil
sea salt and freshly ground black pepper
small handful of chopped chives or parsley
1 teaspoon sherry vinegar

Peel the celeriac and grate it coarsely. Melt the butter in a heavy-based sauté pan with the oil. When it's hot, add the celeriac and cook over a medium heat for 5 minutes, until softened. Season well, add the herbs and sprinkle with the vinegar. Serve.

Sausage Stew with Celeriac and Kale

This is a great one-pan dish, in which you build up the gravy around the ingredients as they cook. Served with good bread, it's a warming winter supper dish. It's fine to use canned beans for stews of this sort but you can soak and cook your beans from scratch. When boiling the beans, it can help them to soften more quickly if you add a pinch of bicarbonate of soda to the water.

Serves 4

500g good pork sausages
100g bacon, cut into lardons
1 tablespoon olive oil
2 onions, sliced
½ celeriac, peeled and chopped into 2cm pieces
2 garlic cloves, crushed
1 sprig of thyme (or a pinch of dried thyme)
1 bay leaf
1 tablespoon tomato purée
100ml red wine
600ml chicken or meat stock
dash of Worcestershire sauce
4 teaspoons Dijon mustard
200g kale, stripped from stalks, shredded
400g tin white beans, rinsed and drained
sea salt and freshly ground black pepper

In a large, heavy-based sauté pan or saucepan, shallow-fry the sausages and lardons in the oil for 5 minutes. Remove the sausages.

Add the onions and cook for 10 minutes. Increase the heat and add the celeriac, stirring frequently to stop the onions from burning. Add the garlic, herbs and tomato purée and stir well for 2 minutes. Deglaze the pan with red wine, stirring to remove the sticky bits from the base, then add the stock, Worcestershire sauce and mustard.

Bring the contents of the pan to a simmer, return the sausages, cover and cook for about 20 minutes. Add the kale to the pan and wilt on top of the other ingredients for 10 minutes, then mix it in. Add the white beans, season and cook for a further 5 minutes.

Beef in Newcastle Brown Ale with Horseradish Dumplings

Ideally, this dish would be made using Double Maxim brown ale – the brew from Sunderland, where I grew up. The brewery at Sunderland is now extinct, so we have had to defect to the other side. In fact, most brown ales will work well (or even Guinness, if you can't get a brown ale). It is worth the extra effort to make the dumplings and the horseradish centre gives them a real kick. You can make the stew the day before eating, reheat and add the dumplings to serve.

Serves 4–6

1kg stewing beef, cut into 2cm cubes
3 tablespoons plain flour, seasoned
2 tablespoons sunflower oil
15g unsalted butter
2 onions, chopped
2 celery sticks, chopped
1 teaspoon English mustard powder, or 1 tablespoon English mustard
1 tablespoon tomato purée
2 teaspoons sugar
1 strip of orange zest
bouquet garni of 1 bay leaf and 1 sprig each of thyme and rosemary, or
    just ½ teaspoon dried thyme
600ml Newcastle Brown Ale
300g carrots, cut into batons
½ swede, cut into batons
½ celeriac, cut into batons (optional)

For the dumplings:
50g breadcrumbs
50g plain flour, plus more to dust
50g suet
½ teaspoon baking powder
sea salt and freshly ground black pepper
big handful of chopped parsley
1 egg, lightly beaten
horseradish relish

Toss the beef in the seasoned flour, then shake off any excess. Heat the oil and butter in a heavy-based pan and fry the beef in batches until slightly browned and sealed. (Do not crowd the pan or the meat will stew.) Remove the meat with a slotted spoon and set aside.

Add the onions and celery to the remaining oil and cook for 5 minutes. Add the rest of the ingredients except the veg and bring to a boil, stirring well and scraping the bottom of the pan to release all the meat 'gubbins'. Return the meat to the pan and make sure it is covered with liquid (if not, add a little water). Cover and simmer over a low heat or in a low oven (140°C/Gas Mark 1) for 2 hours, or until the meat is tender. Mix together all the dry ingredients for the dumplings, season well, then stir in the parsley. Bind with the egg to make a dough and divide into balls about the size of a walnut, rolling them with floured hands. Poke a hole in the side of each, put a little horseradish relish in the hole, then reseal.

Mix the vegetables in with the stew and bring back to a gentle simmer. Place the dumplings on top, cover and simmer for a further 20 minutes.

Francesca's Roast Vegetables with Lime Pickle

From Francesca Melman, another Riverford Cook. This can be the basis of a quick and easy supper, perhaps served with some grilled halloumi cheese. It's a great way to use up any combination of root vegetables: carrots, parsnip, celeriac or swede. You could also add cauliflower, squash or pumpkin.

Serves 4

about 1kg mixed vegetables, peeled if necessary and cut into large chunks
3 tablespoons olive oil
sea salt and freshly ground black pepper
4 tablespoons lime pickle

Preheat the oven to 200°C/Gas Mark 6.

Toss the veg with the oil, salt and pepper and lime pickle and roast in the hot oven until golden and tender. It will take 30–40 minutes.

Tartine Gratinée à l'Oignon

This recipe is from Richard Bertinet, who is now supplying Riverford boxes in some areas with his amazing bread. His sourdough is my favourite and works brilliantly for this dish. Richard's a pretty good cook for a Frenchman, but we felt this recipe just needed anglicising a little so we've added some hot English mustard. Richard's sourdough is also fantastic grilled, rubbed with garlic and used for bruschetta or topped with grilled vegetables.

Serves 4

2 tablespoons olive oil
100g unsalted butter
4 onions, finely sliced
1 teaspoon sugar
30g plain flour
300ml milk
sea salt and freshly ground black pepper
grated nutmeg
100g Gruyère cheese, grated
1 teaspoon English mustard
4 slices good sourdough bread
winter salad leaves, to serve

Preheat the oven to 200°C/Gas Mark 6.

Place the oil and half the butter in a frying pan and put over a low heat. Add the onions and the sugar. Cook over a low heat for about 20 minutes until caramelised.

Make a béchamel: melt the remaining butter in a pan, add the flour and stir to make a roux. Add the milk gradually, stirring all the time. Bring back to a boil and season. Add some grated nutmeg.

Mix the onions, cheese and mustard into the béchamel. Grill the bread slices and lay out on a tray. Divide the onion mixture between them. Bake in the hot oven for 15 minutes. Serve with crisp winter leaves.

Mashed Roots

This is the dish from the Orkneys, known as clapshot. Roughly equal quantities of potato and swede are mashed together with carrot and plenty of butter. It is hearty and versatile. It is a good accompaniment to many meat dishes. Try it as a topping for shepherd's or cottage pie instead of plain potato.

Serves 4–6

350g carrots
450g swede
350g potatoes
75g unsalted butter
85ml milk
sea salt and freshly ground black pepper
grated nutmeg

Boil all the vegetables together, then drain. Add the butter and milk. Mash.

Season with salt, pepper and nutmeg.

Seville Orange Marmalade

Every year my dad used to make marmalade. Apart from scrambled eggs, this was the only cooking he ever did. The recipe below is based on my dad's method, although Guy has perfected and simplified it.

Makes approx. 4kg

1.5kg Seville oranges
2 lemons
approx. 2kg granulated sugar
you will also need: a large pan, muslin, string, sterilised jars, screw-top
    lids or wax discs, cellophane covers and elastic bands

With a sharp knife, peel the skin from the oranges and lemons, leaving as much white pith on the fruit as possible. Chop the peel into 3mm strips and put in a large pan.

Line a large bowl with a piece of muslin. Cut the oranges and lemons in half. With your hands, squeeze the juice from the fruit into the bowl, dropping the leftover squeezed fruit (pith, pips and flesh) into the muslin. Lift the muslin out of the bowl, gather the sides and squeeze any remaining juice into the bowl. Tie the muslin together to keep the fruit in and form a bag. Place the muslin bag in the saucepan with the peel, leaving the top of the muslin overhanging the saucepan. Add the fruit juice and 2.5 litres of cold water. Heat until boiling, then reduce the heat and simmer for 2 hours, until the peel is tender.

Remove the muslin bag and squeeze all the sticky juice from the bag into the pan. Pour the contents of the pan into a measuring jug. Return to the pan and add 450g sugar for every 500ml liquid. Gently heat for 15 minutes, then increase the heat and boil rapidly for 15 minutes. Test whether the marmalade has reached setting point: put a little liquid on a cold saucer and gently push with the back of the spoon. If the liquid starts to wrinkle, setting point has been reached. If not, keep boiling and re-test every 10 minutes. Turn off the heat as soon as you reach setting point.

Leave the mixture to stand for 15 minutes. Stir gently, then carefully spoon into warmed sterilised jars. If using screw-top lids, put the lids on while the marmalade is still hot and turn upside down for 5 minutes to sterilise the lids.

If using cellophane, put a wax disc on the marmalade while warm, then seal with cellophane and an elastic band.

Parsnip and Walnut Beignets

Beignets are deep-fried choux pastry and can be sweet or savoury. These would make a great snack or starter, served with a dip of creamed blue cheese.

Serves 4-6 (as a starter)

400g parsnips, peeled and cut in pieces (woody core removed)
90g butter
1 teaspoon thyme leaves
salt and freshly ground black pepper
1 garlic clove, crushed
50g walnuts, toasted and chopped
200ml milk
80g plain flour, sieved
2 eggs
100g Gruyère cheese, grated
1 tablespoon chopped parsley or chives
sunflower oil, for deep-frying

Preheat the oven to 200°C/Gas Mark 6. Place the parsnips in a baking dish. Melt 30g of the butter and pour it over the parsnips. Add the thyme and seasoning, and toss well. Roast for about 40 minutes or until tender. Remove from the oven, allow to cool slightly, then blend in a food processor with the garlic and walnuts until smooth.

In a small saucepan, melt the remaining 60g butter with the milk and bring up to a simmer. Tip in the flour and beat vigorously until the dough comes away from the side of the pan. Allow to cool, then beat in the eggs, one at a time. Fold in the puréed parsnip, the cheese and parsley or chives. Season well.

Heat 2–3cm oil in a deep pan or deep-fat fryer. Using two dessertspoons, form balls of dough and drop into the hot oil. Fry, in batches if necessary, for about 3–4 minutes until golden brown on all sides.

Red Onion Confit

This is a good way to use up any onions that might be lurking at the bottom of your box; it can also be made using white onions. It takes a little time to make but will keep sealed in the fridge for a couple of weeks. Use it for a quick supper such as simple cheese on toast or a steak sandwich, or for a posh dinner with Duck Confit (see page 45).

Serves 10–12 as a condiment

6 red onions, finely sliced
1 tablespoon olive oil
50g unsalted butter
1 teaspoon sea salt
125ml red wine
2 tablespoons balsamic vinegar
2 tablespoons grenadine (optional)
1 tablespoon soft brown sugar
sea salt and freshly ground black pepper
a little chicken stock, if needed

Cook the onions in the oil and butter with the salt in a heavy-based saucepan over a medium heat for 30 minutes, or until very soft. Add the wine, vinegar, grenadine (if using) and sugar. Simmer over a very low heat for about 45 minutes until most of the liquid has evaporated, stirring occasionally to prevent sticking.

Check and adjust the seasoning. Add a little chicken stock for a more 'saucy' consistency, if you like.

SUNDAY

Warm Pheasant Salad with Pomegranate and Walnuts

I worked briefly at Stephanie Alexander's restaurant in Melbourne, where there was a dish similar to this on the menu. The dressing, in particular, was amazing and I've always tried to recreate it – this is the closest I've got. Pheasant is available from November through to January and it can be bought from good local butchers (they may be able to help you with preparing the birds for this recipe too). Poaching the breast is a good way to stay in control of how quickly it cooks – you don't want to overcook and dry out the meat. If you can't get pumpkin oil, use a nut oil such as walnut or hazelnut instead. Serve with kale and potato cakes, on page 23, or a root vegetable mash.

Serves 4

2 pheasants, legs and breasts removed
about 1 litre chicken stock
1 tablespoon pumpkin oil
1 tablespoon balsamic vinegar
1 teaspoon truffle oil
1 teaspoon soy sauce
seeds from 1 cardamom pod, crushed
sea salt and freshly ground black pepper
100g mixed salad leaves (our Riverford salad bags, at this time of year, generally contain rocket, pak choi, golden mustard, winter purslane, Ashbrooke and dandelion)
seeds from ½ pomegranate
2 tablespoons toasted walnuts

Preheat the oven to 200°C/Gas Mark 6 and roast the pheasant carcasses for 30 minutes until browned. Put in a pan with enough chicken stock to cover them. Bring to a simmer and cook for 1–1½ hours. Then strain the stock and reserve.

Remove the skin from the pheasant legs and simmer in the reserved stock for 1 hour until the leg meat falls off the bone. When cool enough to handle, strip the leg meat and set aside.

Take half the pheasant stock and reduce it to about 200ml. Mix with the pumpkin oil, vinegar, truffle oil, soy sauce and cardamom. Season well and add the leg meat to this dressing.

Remove the skin from the pheasant breasts and poach in the remaining stock until slightly pink, about 10–15 minutes. Remove from the pan and slice.

Warm the leg meat a little in the dressing. Remove the leg meat from the pan and toss with the salad leaves. Arrange on a plate with the sliced poached breasts and sprinkle with the pomegranate seeds and walnuts. Drizzle over the remaining dressing.

Kale and Potato Cakes

A few years ago we had a recipe competition for Riverford customers in the Field Kitchen. Kate Wescombe won with this recipe, which we have adapted slightly over the years, but is now a fixture on the Field Kitchen menu. You can serve it as part of a Sunday lunch or dinner, but if you add a poached egg or grill some strong Cheddar on top, then the cakes could also be a simple weekday supper. If you add a little mashed swede, it becomes something a bit closer to bubble and squeak. Some potato types have a higher moisture content than others. If the mixture feels a bit wet, it might be difficult to pan-fry, so dust the cakes with a little gram flour or plain white flour to prevent them from sticking.

Serves 4

500g baking or large potatoes, cut into large chunks
200g leeks, well washed and finely chopped
75g curly kale, stripped from stalks and finely shredded
50g unsalted butter
2 teaspoons caraway seeds
1 teaspoon paprika
3 teaspoons wholegrain mustard
2 egg yolks
2 tablespoons crème fraîche

Bring the potatoes to a boil in a medium-sized saucepan. Simmer slowly for 30 minutes until cooked. Drain, then mash or put through a potato ricer.

Sauté the leek and kale in a frying pan in half the butter until soft. Add the spices and cook for a further 2 minutes.

Mix together the potato, vegetables, mustard, egg yolks and crème fraîche in a large bowl. Shape into 4 large cakes (or 8 small ones).

Heat the remaining butter in a large frying pan and gently cook the potato cakes on both sides until dark golden and crispy.

Braised Red Cabbage with Beetroot and Orange

I love combining the flavours of orange and caraway – I think it might be my most overused pairing this year. Adding the grated beetroot to the slowly braised cabbage gives the finished dish a deep, glossy purple colour. If you'd like it to look even more sumptuous you can add a knob of butter at the end too. It's important to keep tasting the cabbage as it cooks. You need to be sure the sweet and sour flavours are balanced – add a little more sugar or vinegar as necessary.

Serves 4–6

1 onion, finely chopped
25g unsalted butter, plus 50g more to finish
1 tablespoon olive oil
1 teaspoon caraway seeds
1 red cabbage, cored and finely shredded
finely grated zest and juice of 1 orange
1 tablespoon balsamic vinegar, plus more if needed
1 tablespoon soft brown sugar, plus more if needed
sea salt and freshly ground black pepper
3 beetroot, peeled and finely grated

Cook the onion in the butter and oil for 5 minutes. Add the caraway seeds and, when they start to sizzle, mix in the red cabbage, orange zest and juice, vinegar and sugar. Season well, cover and cook on a low heat for about 45 minutes, stirring occasionally.

Add the beetroot, cover and cook for another 30 minutes. Season well, taste and add more vinegar or sugar to balance the flavours. Stir in the remaining butter for a glossy finish.

Lemon and Orange Tart

January is a fantastic month for oranges: citrus fruit is at its best, while other fruit is limited. This is a variation on a classic lemon tart from the River Café – with the unusual addition of blood oranges. Our blood oranges are grown in the foothills of Mount Etna in Sicily. In the Field Kitchen we also like to use their juice in a cocktail with Campari and prosecco. Serve the tart with crème fraîche.

Serves 10

For the pastry:
175g plain flour, plus more to dust
60g icing sugar
125g unsalted butter, cut into cubes
2 egg yolks

For the filling:
finely grated zest and juice of 3 unwaxed lemons and 3 oranges
    (preferably blood oranges)
250g caster sugar
4 whole eggs
7 egg yolks
220g unsalted butter, softened and chopped
2 teaspoons crème fraîche

Put the flour and icing sugar in a food processor and mix briefly. Add the butter and pulse until the consistency resembles breadcrumbs. Add the egg yolks and pulse until the pastry comes together. Wrap in cling film and leave in the fridge for at least 30 minutes.

Roll out the pastry on a lightly floured surface to about 2mm thick, then use it to line a 24cm loose-bottomed tart tin, pushing the pastry up the sides so it comes slightly above the top of the tin. Chill for 30 minutes. Meanwhile, preheat the oven to 180°C/Gas Mark 4.

Line the pastry case with baking parchment and fill with baking beans or uncooked rice. Bake in the hot oven to 10 minutes, then remove the paper and beans and bake for another 5 minutes, or until golden brown. Remove from the oven and set aside to cool completely.

Increase the oven temperature to 230°C/Gas Mark 8.

Put all the filling ingredients except the crème fraîche in a heavy-based pan and cook over a low heat, gently whisking until the sugar has dissolved and the eggs start to cook (the mixture will thicken). When it is thick enough to coat the back of a spoon, remove from the heat and whisk in the crème fraîche. If you want a very smooth result, push the mixture through a sieve.

Pour the citrus mixture into the cooked tart shell and bake for 6–10 minutes, until the top has slightly browned. Allow to cool before serving.

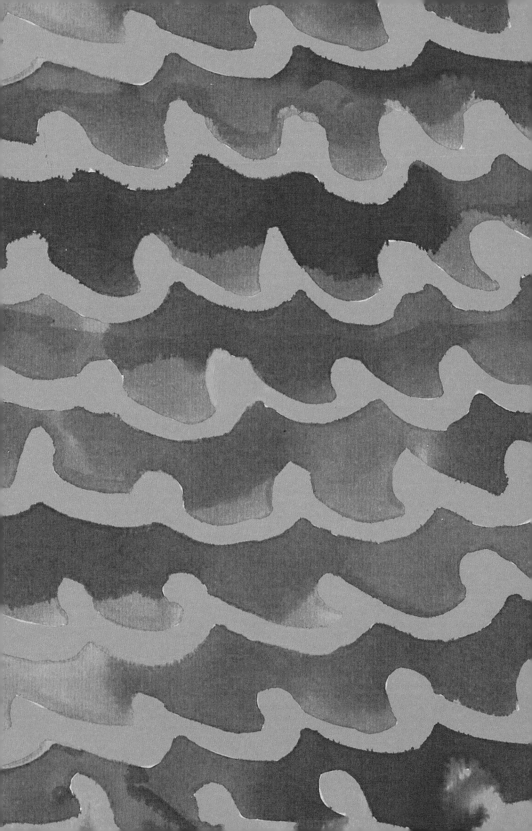

Everyday

Beetroot with Aromatic Spices
Carrots with Cumin and Orange
Cabbage and Sausage Rolls
Spiced Lamb Meatballs with Root Vegetables
Zuppa d'Aosta
Beetroot Dip

Sunday

Duck Confit
Roasted Beetroot and Squash Salad with
Red Onions in a Pistachio Dressing
Middle Eastern Coleslaw
Italian Apple and Honey Cake

FEBRUARY

A glimmer of growth

Things start to wake up towards the end of January. The soil is no warmer, but with light levels rising we start sowing the first seeds under glass. By February there is some renewed vigour in the fields and the first new growth in the remaining leeks, cabbages and kales. Below ground the parsnips start sprouting new roots ready to throw up a seed head. Potatoes and onions, sensing spring, are starting to sprout as soon as they come out of store. In domestic kitchens, roots that were fine in a cool vegetable rack through autumn and early winter also begin to sprout. You can slow this down by keeping them in the fridge. Like our vegetables, we too are longing for spring. We start looking for dry windows in the weather to start muck spreading, ploughing and making seedbeds ready for the first outdoor sowings and plantings. By the end of the month, if conditions are favourable, we will risk planting out the first cabbage and some early potatoes on south-facing slopes, usually protected by fleece crop covers.

Still a long way to go

While we are getting impatient for spring, we hope that the nation's veg box cooks are not. We still have a long way to go before the first crops are ready for harvest in May and June and there's a lot of hearty winter veg still to be eaten. I think a confident cook should be able to maintain an interesting diet on at least 90 per cent local veg. The splendid Savoys will come to an end and we then have a run of round 'tundra' cabbage, supplemented by some spring greens (wonderfully sweet and tender, loose-hearted, immature cabbages typically weighing 100 to 200 grams). By now we are arguing with the pigeons over any surviving greenery. We both favour the spring greens so lead is often called on to settle the dispute. Seared pigeon breast on a bed of winter leaves with a nutty dressing provides compensation (for us) for their ill-advised pecking.

Cauliflowers, lightweight moaners and a few pragmatic peppers

Groans from our veg box customers about unending roots, leeks, kale, cauliflower and cabbage normally surface by the end of the month and we ignore these for as long as we dare. We are still trying to keep imports to a minimum, saving them for the next two months when things get really lean. The quality of greens from the fields and roots from store is generally good, but it is all starting to get a bit tedious for the worldly 21st-century cook, and by the end of the month we are getting regular shipments from our two favourite Spanish growers. If we were completely hard-line about

imports (as many of our customers tell us they would like us to be), I would have gone bust by now. Rather than sacrificing ourselves on the cross of localism, and becoming martyrs to a much-touted ideal that few live up to in practice, for the last few years we have been nursing our customers through the winter with the occasional pepper, tomato, cucumber or bean from two growers in Andalucía. There is the philosophical, charming, idealistic but not always reliable Paco from Motril who, with a group of small local growers along the coast, is always ready to try new crops and ways of growing them, including even bananas. In addition to flat beans and peppers, he supplies us with wonderful Hass avocados (the black crinkly ones: the only ones worth buying) from November to April, and some great mangoes earlier in the winter. We know him as wacko Paco to distinguish him from our other Paco up the coast north of Almería who, rather more reliably and less philosophically, supplies tomatoes, aubergine and Ramiro peppers.

These panderings to human weakness and commercial pragmatism notwithstanding, February is too early to abandon local vegetables and pretend winter is over. Beetroot, carrots and celeriac are still storing well and when added to the other roots and greens from our fields provide huge scope for warming roasts, stews with the occasional winter beetroot or celeriac salad as a nod to the increasing elevation of the sun.

Quick and easy ideas
KALE

Kale and potatoes

Cook chopped onion and garlic in a little oil in a large pan until softened. Add a few diced potatoes and cover with ham stock or chicken stock. Simmer for 15 minutes. Add shredded kale and cook for a few more minutes until wilted. Season and serve with sausages.

Kale with tomato and capers

Cook sliced onion and garlic in a little oil in a large pan for a few minutes. Add shredded kale with 50ml hot water and cook uncovered for about 5 minutes. Add 200ml tomato passata, a splash of wine vinegar, a small handful of capers and a drizzle of honey. Season and simmer for 20 minutes.

A pasta sauce with kale

Cook 4 thinly sliced garlic cloves in 2 tablespoons olive oil with 2 chopped dried chillies. Before the garlic starts to brown, add shredded kale and cook quickly until wilted. Thinly slice semi-dried or sun-dried tomatoes and add to the kale with a small handful of toasted pine nuts or flaked almonds. Cover and cook for 5 minutes. Season well. Toss through cooked pasta and sprinkle with coarsely grated hard ricotta, feta or pecorino cheese.

Kale and polenta

Add chopped cooked kale to wet polenta to make a colourful alternative to mash, stir in Parmesan and butter and serve with a braise or stew.

Braised kale with chickpeas or lentils

When braising kale, chuck in some leftover chopped salami, chopped chilli and a pinch of ground fennel. This can be finished with a few tablespoons of cooked chickpeas, beans or lentils.

EVERYDAY

Beetroot with Aromatic Spices

Curry spices revive root vegetables that have been stored over winter, and this is a great recipe for the older beetroot available at this time of year. It's a popular recipe with our box customers, as it's a variation on roasting or baking their beetroot. Serve simply with basmati rice and yoghurt.

Serves 2

2 tablespoons groundnut or sunflower oil
½ teaspoon black mustard seeds
1 onion, thinly sliced
2 garlic cloves, crushed or finely chopped
1–2 chillies, deseeded if preferred, finely chopped
2 curry leaves, or 1 bay leaf
½ teaspoon ground coriander
1 teaspoon ground cumin
¼ teaspoon turmeric
¼ teaspoon ground cinnamon
500g raw beetroot, peeled and cut into 2cm pieces
2 tomatoes, chopped, or 200g tinned tomatoes
sea salt and freshly ground black pepper
100ml coconut milk
juice of 1 lime
handful of coriander leaves, chopped (optional)

In a wok or large pan, heat the oil and add the mustard seeds. When they start to pop, add the onion, garlic and chillies and fry until the onion is soft. Add the rest of the spices and the beetroot and fry for another couple of minutes.

Add the tomatoes and 200ml water. Season with salt and pepper to taste. Simmer for 30–45 minutes, stirring every now and then, until the beetroot is tender.

Add the coconut milk and simmer for another couple of minutes, until the sauce has thickened. Stir in the lime juice and add more salt and pepper to taste. Add the coriander leaves (if using) just before serving.

Carrots with Cumin and Orange

Orange works well with carrot. We often use orange and cumin in the dressing for raw carrot salads. Here, instead, the carrot is braised with the seasonings, and the final dish has a slightly Moroccan flavour. You can serve with Chermoulah Chicken (see page 254) or even add the Tahini Dressing (see page 175).

Serves 4–6

2 tablespoons sunflower oil
800g carrots, thinly sliced
2 garlic cloves, crushed
2 tablespoons cumin seeds, dry-roasted in a pan for 3 minutes
2 teaspoons sugar
1 bay leaf
1 sprig of thyme
zest and juice of 4 oranges
sea salt and freshly ground black pepper
25g butter

In a large frying pan, heat the oil over a moderate heat until hot. Add the carrots, garlic, cumin and sugar. Pour in enough water to come halfway up the depth of the carrots – about 400ml – and add the bay leaf and thyme. Cover, bring to a boil and simmer for about 15 minutes, or until the carrots are quite soft.

Add the orange zest and juice, turn up the heat and cook uncovered for another 10 minutes, or until the liquid has evaporated, stirring occasionally. Season and stir in the butter before serving.

Cabbage and Sausage Rolls

The idea for the filling in this recipe came from the best sausage rolls I've ever eaten, sold in a shop called Lynn's in Apia, Samoa. The bus would stop right outside and everyone would rush into the shop to buy them. I decided to create a healthier version using cabbage leaves instead of pastry.

Makes 6–8 rolls

1 head Savoy cabbage, or other green cabbage
sea salt and freshly ground black pepper
2 onions, finely chopped
2 celery sticks, finely chopped
25g unsalted butter, plus more for the dish
1 tablespoon olive oil
2 garlic cloves, crushed
500g good-quality sausagemeat
1 tablespoon wholegrain mustard
1 teaspoon Worcestershire sauce
1 apple, peeled and finely grated
1 tablespoon chopped parsley and/or chives

Preheat the oven to 160°C/Gas Mark 3.

Remove any damaged tough outer leaves from the cabbage and discard. Take off the next 6–8 leaves and put to one side. Finely shred the rest of the cabbage, discarding the core. Blanch the whole leaves in boiling salted water for 1 minute, drain, remove the thick central rib from each and lay out flat.

Cook the onions and celery in the butter and oil for 10 minutes until soft. Add the garlic and cook for 1 minute. Add the shredded cabbage, increase the heat and stir for a few minutes to wilt the cabbage. Remove from the heat and allow to cool. In a bowl, mix the shredded cabbage and onion with the sausagemeat, mustard, Worcestershire sauce, apple and herbs. Season well.

Divide the filling between the cabbage leaves, shaping each portion into a sausage. Roll up into a parcel, folding in the ends so the filling is completely covered. Butter an oven dish in which all the parcels will fit snugly. Season, cover tightly and bake for about 1 hour, until they are firm to the touch.

Spiced Lamb Meatballs with Root Vegetables

Don't be put off by the length of the ingredients list – this dish is really quick to put together and a good way to use up any root vegetables left at the bottom of your veg box. It can be served without the root vegetable sauce, though. You could eat it simply with a tomato sauce, or with Aromatic Pumpkin (see page 296) and couscous.

Serves 4–6

1 onion, finely chopped
3 tablespoons olive oil
2 garlic cloves, crushed
1 red chilli, deseeded if preferred, chopped
750g minced lamb
½ teaspoon ground fennel seeds
1 teaspoon paprika
1 teaspoon ground cumin
1 teaspoon ground coriander
2 tablespoons soft breadcrumbs
1 egg
1 tablespoon chopped coriander or mint, plus more to serve (optional)
sea salt and freshly ground black pepper

For the sauce:
1 onion, finely sliced
2 garlic cloves, finely sliced
pinch of saffron strands
pinch of chilli powder
400g tin chopped tomatoes
1 teaspoon sugar
200ml red wine
200ml chicken stock
1 cinnamon stick
750g root vegetables, cut into 1cm cubes (swede, turnip, parsnip and
    celeriac)

For the meatballs, cook the onion in 1 tablespoon of the oil for about 10 minutes until soft, then add the garlic and chilli. Cook for another minute,

then remove from the heat and allow to cool. Mix well with the rest of the meatball ingredients. Roll into balls about the size of golf balls.

In a large, deep frying pan, brown off the meatballs in the remaining oil. Remove from the pan with a slotted spoon.

For the sauce, add the onion, garlic, saffron and chilli powder to the pan, place over a low heat and cook for 10 minutes, then add the tomatoes and sugar. Increase the heat and cook for 5 minutes, then add the wine, stock and cinnamon stick. Bring to a simmer and add the root vegetables. Mix well and simmer for 10 minutes.

Return the meatballs to the pan and cook for a further 10 minutes until the sauce has thickened, the vegetables are tender and the meatballs are cooked through.

Season and finish with a sprinkling of coriander or mint (if using).

Zuppa d'Aosta

This soup comes from the Aosta valley in northern Italy, where hearty dishes, often involving melted Fontina cheese, dominate the local food because of the cooler climate. I think the anchovies are vital to the flavour of the finished dish. Savoy cabbages are abundant in January and February and work well in this dish, but you could make it with any other kind of green cabbage.

Serves 6

1 Savoy cabbage, cored and shredded
12–15 1–2cm slices of ciabatta or similar bread (approx. 300g)
1 garlic clove, halved
12–15 anchovies
125g Fontina or Emmental cheese, grated
2 tablespoons grated Parmesan cheese
sea salt and freshly ground black pepper
1.25 litres good chicken stock

Preheat the oven to 170°C/Gas Mark 4.

Blanch the shredded cabbage in boiling water for 3 minutes. Drain and refresh in cold water, then drain again.

Griddle the slices of ciabatta in a grill pan for a minute on each side. Rub each piece with the cut garlic clove.

Layer up the ingredients in a deep ovenproof pan or casserole dish, starting with a little cabbage, then bread, placing an anchovy on each slice, then the Fontina or Emmental. Repeat, so there are three layers of bread and cabbage. Finish with any remaining Fontina or Emmental and the Parmesan. Season the stock well, unless using ready-made, and pour it down the side of the dish. Bake, uncovered, in the hot oven for about 30 minutes.

Beetroot Dip

This dip was created by Rob Andrew, who worked with us in Riverford's Travelling Field Kitchen, which toured the country in a yurt last summer, and who now runs our staff canteen. If you have leftover baked or roast beetroot, just omit the first part of the method, and add the sugar and balsamic vinegar before puréeing.

Serves 4

olive oil
knob of unsalted butter
1kg beetroot, peeled and chopped
splash of balsamic vinegar
sea salt and freshly ground black pepper
pinch of dark brown sugar
1–2 teaspoons ground cumin
2 tablespoons yoghurt or crème fraîche

Heat a little oil and butter in a large pan. When the butter is foaming and starts to turn brown, add the beetroot. Stir and add the balsamic vinegar, salt and pepper to taste and a dash of water. Place a tight-fitting lid on the pan and let the beetroot steam until tender. Keep checking every 10 minutes or so to make sure the beetroot doesn't catch at the bottom, and add a little more water if the pan is boiling dry. Add the sugar.

Purée the beetroot in a food processor or with a stick blender until smooth. Add cumin to taste and more salt and pepper if needed.

Add the yoghurt or crème fraîche just before serving, stirring in well.

SUNDAY

Duck Confit

We serve this in the Field Kitchen along with the duck breasts, cooked rare. Once the legs are cooked in the fat they will keep for a couple of weeks in the fridge, and can be taken out for a quick supper. The duck can be used in a variety of dishes. Try serving it shredded and crispy, with cucumber, in Chinese pancakes or in the Hispi Cabbage dish on page 184.

Makes 6 pieces

3 tablespoons sea salt
1 teaspoon ground black peppercorns
leaves from 1 large sprig of thyme
1 garlic clove, finely chopped, plus 1 garlic bulb, halved horizontally
1 bay leaf, crumbled
zest of 1 orange
6 duck legs
750ml duck fat, or good-quality lard, or goose fat

Mix the salt with the pepper, thyme, chopped garlic, bay and orange zest. Toss the duck legs with the salt mix. Lay in a tray, cover and leave in the fridge for at least 12 hours or overnight. Preheat the oven to 120°C/Gas Mark ½. Remove the duck legs from the salt, rub off any excess and pat dry with a clean cloth.

Arrange the duck legs in an ovenproof dish in which they will sit snugly. Spoon the fat over and add the halved bulb of garlic. Cover and cook in the oven for 1½–2 hours, until the legs are tender and the meat is falling from the bone. Allow to cool.

The duck legs can now either be placed in the fridge in the pan they were cooked in, or removed from the fat to a more suitable container, then re-covered with the fat. They will keep for 2 weeks and the flavours will deepen.

To use, remove the duck legs from the fat and scrape off any excess into a non-stick, oven-proof frying pan placed over a medium heat. When hot, add the duck confit skin-side down and cook for a few minutes. Turn over and transfer to a hot oven for 5 minutes.

45

Roasted Beetroot and Squash Salad with Red Onions in a Pistachio Dressing

This is a fresh and colourful dish for the dark days of February. It uses stored squash and beetroot but you could substitute other sweet vegetables, such as carrots or parsnips. I prefer to roast the beetroot whole, in their skins, as I think they taste best and are easy to peel that way. But, if you prefer, you could peel them first and cut them up into pieces to roast. Serve this salad at room temperature.

Serves 6

6 beetroot
sea salt and freshly ground black pepper
3 tablespoons olive oil
700g squash
½ red onion, thinly sliced
1 tablespoon balsamic vinegar
2 teaspoons light muscovado sugar
2 oranges, peeled and segmented
75g feta cheese

For the dressing:
150g shelled unsalted pistachios
grated zest and juice of 1 orange
1 red chilli, deseeded if preferred, chopped
1 garlic clove, crushed
1 tablespoon balsamic vinegar
4 tablespoons olive oil
1 tablespoon chopped parsley or coriander
sea salt and freshly ground black pepper

Preheat the oven to 200°C/Gas Mark 6. Put the beetroot in a tray with a little water, salt, pepper and 1 tablespoon of the olive oil, cover with foil and roast for about 1 hour. When cool enough to handle, peel and cut into eighths.

At the same time, cut the squash in half lengthways, remove the seeds, then peel and slice it across into pieces about 1cm thick. Place on a roasting tray and drizzle with 1 tablespoon more olive oil, and roast for about 30 minutes until tender.

Meanwhile, place the red onion, balsamic vinegar and sugar in a small bowl, mix well, and set aside for 30 minutes to marinate.

Make the pistachio dressing by toasting the pistachios lightly in a medium oven or in a small frying pan, then cool. Chop roughly and mix with all the other ingredients.

Toss the beetroot and squash in the remaining 1 tablespoon olive oil and add the marinated onions. Season with salt and pepper to taste. Add the oranges and drizzle with the pistachio dressing. To finish, crumble feta cheese over the top.

Middle Eastern Coleslaw

Sumac can be hard to get hold of, but it is becoming more popular and should be available from Middle Eastern and good spice shops. There is a trick to getting the seeds out of a pomegranate – cut it in half and take one half in your hand, cut-side down. Give it a good bash on the skin side (perhaps use a wooden spoon) and all the seeds should fall out easily.

Serves 4–6

1 red onion, finely sliced
1 tablespoon balsamic vinegar
2 teaspoons brown sugar
2 tablespoons sultanas
½ red cabbage, cored and finely shredded
¼ white cabbage, cored and finely shredded
1 carrot, grated
3 tablespoons olive oil
zest and juice of 2 oranges
2 teaspoons sumac
sea salt and freshly ground black pepper
1 tablespoon chopped coriander leaves
2 tablespoons pine nuts, toasted
seeds from 1 pomegranate

Place the onion, vinegar and sugar in a small bowl, mix, and leave to soak for 30 minutes. At the same time, cover the sultanas with hot water and leave them to soak too.

Mix together both the cabbages, the carrot and onion mixture in a bowl. Whisk together the oil, orange juice and zest and sumac and season well.

Toss the dressing with the cabbage and all the other ingredients in a bowl.

Italian Apple and Honey Cake

Assembling this cake might look a bit fiddly, but if you have all your ingredients ready it is simply a process of building up the layers. It really is worth it, as the result is a lovely moist cake. It's quite a flexible recipe – we've replaced the figs with prunes and the pine nuts with almonds before – and it can also work well as a gluten-free pudding: simply use rice flour with gluten-free baking powder instead of self-raising flour in the batter.

Serves 10–12

knob of soft unsalted butter, for the tin
1 tablespoon ground almonds
1kg good eating apples, cored and finely sliced
100g pine nuts, toasted
150g dried figs, chopped
100g light muscovado sugar
100g caster sugar
3 eggs
100ml milk
150g self-raising flour, sifted

For the topping:
50g muscovado sugar
1 tablespoon icing sugar
1 teaspoon ground cinnamon

For the honey syrup:
1 tablespoon honey
juice of 1 lemon

Preheat the oven to 150°C/Gas Mark 2.

Line a 24cm springform cake tin with baking parchment. Butter the paper and scatter in the ground almonds, tipping and shaking the tin until the paper is evenly covered.

Layer a third of the apples in the bottom of the tin. Sprinkle a third of the pine nuts and figs on top.

Beat the sugars and eggs until pale and light. Add the milk, then fold in the flour. Pour half this batter on top of the apples.

Layer another third of the apples, figs and pine nuts on top of the batter. Pour over the remaining batter, then finally place on the remaining apples, figs and pine nuts.

Mix all the ingredients for the sugar topping together, and sprinkle over the cake.

Bake for 1 hour 20 minutes, until firm to the touch and a skewer inserted into the centre comes out clean.

When the cake is cooked, bring the honey to a boil, stir in the lemon juice and pour this syrup evenly over the cake.

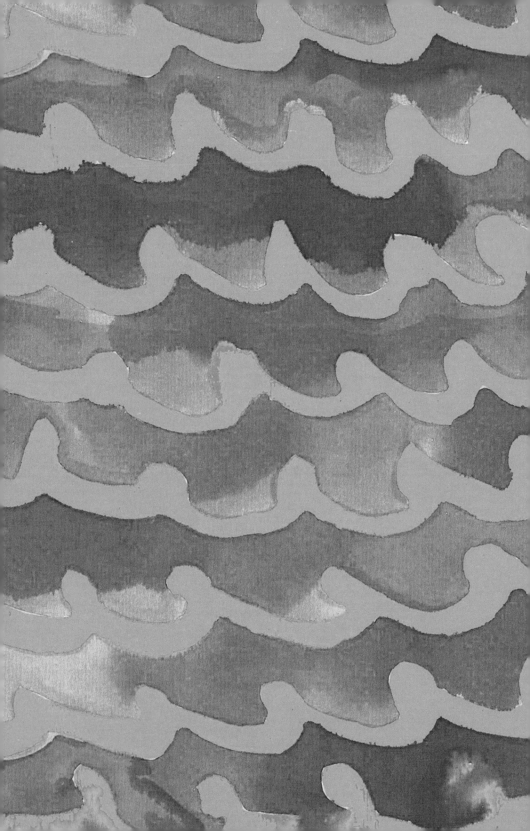

Everyday

Quick Roasted Cauliflower Cheese
Cabbage, Bacon and Potatoes
Spiced Cauliflower
Quick Braised Cauliflower
Cauliflower Soup with Truffle Oil and Parmesan
Baked Potato Fillings
Coconut Pancakes with Mango and Prawns
Caper and Tarragon Dressing

Sunday

Purple Sprouting Broccoli and Kale in a Mustard Dressing
Roast Pork Belly
Kale Gratin
Lime Cheesecake with Pineapple and Mango

MARCH

Into the hungry gap

March marks the start of the descent into the 'hungry gap', an annual challenge for the most loyal of Riverford's veg box customers. The variety of local vegetables progressively declines as both crops from store and those that have over-wintered in the fields reach the end of their seasons. There are still good vegetables to be had but there is less variety and it tends to be the same old stuff we have been eating all winter. We have been planting for a month but even with crop covers and our mild climate nothing is growing very fast; it will be another two months before there are any new season crops to pick. No one will starve as there are still plenty of winter roots and greens around to make a balanced meal, but winter is starting to drag on and we find all but the most hard-line veg box enthusiasts start reaching, with increasing frequency, for the peppers, tomatoes and occasional convenience salad from Spain.

Localism, carbon footprints, anguish and compromise ●
Should we indulge such lightweights and get trucking, or should we lecture on carbon footprints and tell them to eat our swede or go back to the supermarket? Our studies suggest that, in carbon terms at least, the hard-liners may be getting a rash from that horse-hair shirt for nothing. There are other reasons to support local food but it is not always best for the environment, especially if heat has been used to bring crops forward. Local tomatoes, peppers, cucumbers or courgettes in March will have been produced using large amounts of heat and are almost always an environmental disaster. Ideally, we would just wait until June for the unheated local ones, but whatever the public protestations, a survey of the nation's fridges (out of professional interest I always sneak a look when visiting friends) reveals that very few people follow through in private. Our pragmatic compromise is a share in a farm 250 road miles south, in the coastal Vendée just south of the Loire (closer to Devon than the Fens). Despite being so close, it is one of the earliest cropping regions in France: about six weeks ahead of the UK, reducing a two-month hungry gap to a mild culinary inconvenience, at, I would argue, a tolerable environmental cost. We will be cutting our first lettuce and perhaps some spinach by the end of March to give some relief from parsnips and swede. More contentiously, we also work with two growers in Andalucía and one in Italy to source the crops we cannot grow in the Vendée. For those who want to eat tomatoes and peppers in March (I'm afraid that is at least 90 per cent of us), our calculations suggest it takes up to ten times less energy to truck from Spain than to grow in heated glass in the UK.

Purple sprouting rules

Stay off the Spanish broccoli if you can. Calabrese broccoli is all imported (normally from Spain and Italy) from November to June. I am ashamed to say we even import a little ourselves, such is the nation's insatiable and, to me, unfathomable affection for the stuff. Our local, hardy, frost-tolerant version, purple sprouting broccoli, is so much sweeter and more interesting to eat, so try to save your carbon footprint for the tomatoes. The season for PSB (as it is known on the farm) starts slowly in December and reaches a peak in quality and volume in late March, when the most tender varieties are cropping. PSB has not been as intensively bred as the boringly uniform, pathetically frost-tender 'calabrese' broccoli (originally from Calabria in southern Italy). It is more variable in size, shape and heading date. This means we have to walk the field up to ten times to pick the whole crop; hence it tends to be more expensive. Intensive selection for a small number of quantifiable traits within a breeding programme invariably brings yield and uniformity at the price of flavour, hardiness and, I suspect, nutritional content. PSB takes a bit more preparation – you may need to peel larger, older stalks but don't throw away the small leaves around the head. Work around a head slicing each floret and a section of stalk of similar thickness so they cook in the same time.

Inspiring leeks and cauliflower

With the sun climbing and the equinox passing we start seeing flushes of good-quality growth from the remaining cauliflower, leeks and spring greens to accompany the purple sprouting broccoli as it reaches its peak. There are still lots of good vegetables to be had and I would urge cooks to make the most of them before reaching for imports. As we emerge from winter and yearn for something lighter, you might find inspiration by looking south and east: spiced or tempura-fried cauliflower; purple sprouting broccoli and cauliflower with a mustard dressing; griddled leeks and vinaigrette – there is still plenty of potential on our doorstep for the imaginative cook. Having said that, I wouldn't feel too bad about the occasional, thoughtfully sourced import, provided it tastes of something when it gets here.

Quick and easy ideas
PURPLE SPROUTING BROCCOLI

Blanching

To blanch purple sprouting broccoli, add to a pan of boiling water for 3 minutes. Drain and refresh immediately in cold water to stop any further cooking and to preserve the colour, then drain again.

Griddled purple sprouting broccoli

Blanch then griddle on a griddle plate and serve with a poached egg, shredded ham and hollandaise sauce.

Purple sprouting broccoli in a stir-fry

Stir-fry finely sliced rump steak or chicken, then add blanched purple sprouting broccoli. Finish with fresh chilli and oyster sauce.

Spicy greens

Cook chopped chilli, garlic and onion in a little oil. Add blanched chopped broccoli and any cooked greens (including peas). Stir together and cook until heated through. I used to make this in the Solomon Islands, adding tinned chilli tuna (sustainable, line-caught tuna, of course); make your own version with tinned tuna, sweet chilli sauce and some vinegar. A handful of fresh basil or coriander makes this dish even better.

Purple sprouting broccoli with butter and pecorino

Toss blanched purple sprouting broccoli in foaming melted butter, season and toss through grated Parmesan or pecorino.

Quick Roasted Cauliflower Cheese

We've stopped boiling cauliflower in the Field Kitchen – we either roast it in the oven or braise it. It cooks very quickly in the oven, its flavour is intensified and it is a million miles away from the soggy cauliflower that many people have bad memories of being forced to eat. This is a quick, less fussy version of the classic cauliflower cheese. It avoids the béchamel sauce, and instead uses crème fraîche to bind everything together. It tastes wonderful and, even better, there's very little washing up – in fact, you can mix everything in the baking dish if you like. It can be a warming side dish or a simple supper on its own. You could add leeks or bacon.

Serves 4–6

1 cauliflower, cut into florets
1 tablespoon olive oil
1 teaspoon caster sugar
sea salt and freshly ground black pepper
250g crème fraîche
1 teaspoon Dijon mustard
100g Gruyère cheese, grated
1 tablespoon grated Parmesan cheese
handful of chopped chives (optional)

Preheat the oven to 180°C/Gas Mark 4.

Toss the cauliflower in the oil and sugar, season well and roast on a baking tray for 20 minutes, or until just cooked, then empty into a bowl. Increase the oven temperature to 200°C/Gas Mark 6.

Mix the crème fraîche with the mustard and half the Gruyère and season. Mix in the cauliflower until coated and transfer to an ovenproof serving dish. Sprinkle with the rest of the Gruyère and the Parmesan and bake in the hot oven for 10 minutes until golden. Sprinkle with chives (if using).

Cabbage, Bacon and Potatoes

This recipe is based on the traditional French tartiflette. It can be quite a heavy dish, but adding cabbage lightens it, and introduces a little variation in texture. Use crème fraîche in place of the single cream if you prefer. Serve with crusty bread and early salad leaves for a simple warming meal.

Serves 4–6

750g slightly waxy potatoes (at this time of year we usually have Valor from store), cut into small pieces
sea salt and freshly ground black pepper
1 onion, finely chopped
100g smoked streaky bacon lardons
1 tablespoon olive oil
15g unsalted butter
100ml white wine
100ml single cream
½ Savoy cabbage, cored and shredded
200g Gruyère or other melting cheese
1 tablespoon chopped chives (optional)

Preheat the oven to 190°C/Gas Mark 5.

Parboil the potatoes for 10 minutes in boiling salted water. Drain. Cook the onion and bacon in the oil and butter for 10 minutes in a large frying pan over a medium heat, until soft but not coloured. Add the wine and potatoes and cook for about 10 minutes or until tender, stirring all the time. Add the cream and cabbage, cook for another minute, then season and set aside.

Lay half the potato mixture in an ovenproof dish and sprinkle with half the cheese. Repeat with the rest of the mixture. Bake in the hot oven for about 20 minutes. Sprinkle with chives (if using) before serving.

Spiced Cauliflower

The method for this recipe is essentially the same as for the Quick Braised Cauliflower. Cauliflower marries really well with Indian spices, particularly mustard seed, and absorbs their flavours easily. Serve with basmati rice to make a more substantial meal.

Serves 4–6

1 tablespoon sunflower oil
15g unsalted butter
1 teaspoon ground coriander
1 teaspoon ground cumin
pinch of turmeric
1 teaspoon brown mustard seeds
1 onion, thinly sliced
1 garlic clove, crushed
2cm piece fresh root ginger, finely chopped
1 cauliflower, cut into florets
1 teaspoon caster sugar
sea salt and freshly ground black pepper
1 tablespoon chopped coriander leaves (optional)

Heat the oil and butter in a pan large enough to hold the cauliflower in one layer. Add the spices, onion, garlic and ginger to the pan. When the mustard seeds start to pop quickly add the cauliflower, stirring vigorously. Add the sugar, season well, cover and reduce the heat. Leave for 10 minutes on a gentle simmer. Uncover, and check the cauliflower is tender. Stir again, cover, remove from the heat and leave to finish cooking for 10 minutes in its own steam.

Check the seasoning and sprinkle with coriander (if using) to serve.

Quick Braised Cauliflower

In this recipe the cauliflower is cooked slowly in its own juices with saffron and paprika, so that the flavour and colour of the spices are absorbed into the vegetable. It's best to use a pan large enough for the cauliflower to fit in one layer so the florets get equal exposure to the heat. A large sauté pan would be ideal.

Serves 4–6

pinch of saffron strands
1 tablespoon raisins
2 tablespoons olive oil
1 cauliflower, cut into florets
2 tablespoons flaked almonds
1 garlic clove, crushed
½ teaspoon paprika
sea salt and freshly ground black pepper
handful of chopped mint and parsley (optional)
1 teaspoon sherry vinegar

Soak the saffron strands in 3 tablespoons boiling water. Soak the raisins in enough boiling water to cover.

Heat the oil in a large saucepan, add the cauliflower, almonds and garlic and stir-fry for 5 minutes until browned. Add the saffron with its water and the paprika. Mix well. Cover and leave to cook gently for 10–15 minutes, or until the cauliflower is tender.

Drain the raisins of any excess water, mix them into the cauliflower, season well and finish with the herbs (if using) and vinegar.

Cauliflower Soup with Truffle Oil and Parmesan

This is a delicious soup, combining the fresh flavour of cauliflower with the stronger taste of truffle oil. Serve as soon as the soup is ready – that fresh quality of the cauliflower is lost very quickly. Some people aren't fans of truffle oil, but I think it works brilliantly with both cauliflower and Jerusalem artichoke. Some truffle oils can taste synthetic so, as you'll only use a small amount, it's worth spending a bit of money on a good-quality one.

Serves 4

1 onion, finely chopped
1 tablespoon olive oil
25g unsalted butter
2 garlic cloves, crushed
1 cauliflower, cut into florets
sea salt and freshly ground black pepper
200ml milk
drizzle of truffle oil
1 tablespoon grated Parmesan cheese

Cook the onion slowly in the oil and butter in a large saucepan over a low heat for 15 minutes, without colouring, then add the garlic and cook for another 2 minutes. Tip in the cauliflower, increase the heat and cook for 5 minutes, stirring continuously so it is well combined. Season, reduce the heat and cover. Allow to cook gently for another 10 minutes or until the cauliflower becomes soft. Add the milk and bring to a simmer. Season again, then drizzle in a little truffle oil and half the Parmesan.

Blitz in a food processor or a liquidiser, or using a stick blender, while still hot. Pass through a sieve. Serve immediately, drizzled with more oil and scattered with the remaining Parmesan.

Baked Potato Fillings

This is a really simple meal and an easy way to tart up plain potatoes. It's a version of something my mum used to make, she filled her potatoes with bacon and cheese.

Enough for 4 baked potatoes

Bake your potatoes as normal, then remove from the oven. Cut off a 'lid' and scoop out the flesh. Mix the potato flesh with one of the fillings below, then spoon it back into the potato jackets and return to the oven.

For the leek and mustard filling:
2 leeks, well washed and finely chopped
2 tablespoons olive oil
2 tablespoons wholegrain mustard
125g Cheddar cheese, grated
3 tablespoons double cream
handful of chopped parsley
knob of unsalted butter
sea salt and freshly ground black pepper

Cook the leeks in the olive oil in a frying pan over a medium heat for 10 minutes without browning. Add to the potato flesh, mashing well. Add the rest of the ingredients and season. Return to the potato jackets and bake for 5–6 minutes.

For the smoked fish and horseradish filling:
2 egg yolks
4 tablespoons soured cream
2 tablespoons creamed horseradish
150g smoked mackerel fillet, or similar
handful of chopped parsley or chives
sea salt and freshly ground black pepper
sprinkle of cayenne pepper

Put all the ingredients except the cayenne pepper in a bowl with the potato flesh, mix well and season. Return to the potato jackets, sprinkle with cayenne pepper and bake for 5–6 minutes.

Coconut Pancakes with Mango and Prawns

These pancakes, based on a recipe in Leslie Forbes's book *Remarkable Feasts*, are northern Thai street food. I've added mango to the filling. We import both mangoes and pineapples at this time of year, before the UK rhubarb and soft fruit become available. The pancakes are quick enough to make for supper and can be reheated (or the batter can be made and kept in the fridge) but they are also glam enough for a starter or canapé.

Serves 10 as a starter, or makes about 30 canapés

For the pancakes:
90g creamed coconut
150g rice flour
50g gram flour
1 large egg, beaten
1 teaspoon sea salt
1 teaspoon turmeric
1 tablespoon brown sugar
juice of 2 limes

For the prawn and mango filling:
90g desiccated coconut
250g raw prawns, peeled and deveined
1 tablespoon chopped coriander leaves
2 garlic cloves, crushed
2 red chillies, deseeded if preferred, chopped
2 tablespoons sunflower oil
1 teaspoon sea salt
1 teaspoon freshly ground black pepper
2 teaspoons fish sauce
1 tablespoon brown sugar
1 mango (ripe), finely diced

For the pancake batter, mix the creamed coconut with 350ml boiling water to make a smooth paste and set aside. Mix together the flours and egg in a food processor, gradually adding the creamed coconut. Then stir in all the remaining ingredients. The batter should have the consistency of double cream; you may have to add some hot water if it seems a little thick. Set aside and allow to rest for 1 hour.

For the filling, cover the desiccated coconut with boiling water and set aside to soak for 30 minutes. Squeeze out the excess water. Grind together the prawns and coconut in a food processor. Fry the coriander leaves, garlic and chillies in the sunflower oil for 2 minutes over a medium heat. Add the prawns and coconut and continue cooking for 10 minutes until the prawns are cooked. Season, add the fish sauce and brown sugar, then add the mango.

In a non-stick pan, cook the pancakes in batches by dropping in a dessertspoon of batter at a time and spreading it out with the back of a spoon. The pancakes should have a yellow, lacy appearance. Turn over after 3 minutes to cook the other side. Remove from the pan and top with a little of the mango filling.

Caper and Tarragon Dressing

The idea for this comes from dragoncello, the coarse Italian salsa usually served with bollito misto. We like to serve it with roast cauliflower, grilled leeks or baked potatoes.

Serves 6

2 eggs, hard-boiled and chopped
1 tablespoon chopped capers
2 tablespoons chopped tarragon
2 tablespoons chopped parsley
½ red onion, finely chopped
1 tablespoon red wine vinegar
4 tablespoons extra virgin olive oil
1 teaspoon Dijon mustard
1 garlic clove, crushed
sea salt and freshly ground black pepper

Mix all the ingredients together to make a rough salsa.

SUNDAY

Purple Sprouting Broccoli and Kale in a Mustard Dressing

The mustard seeds bring an interesting flavour and texture to this dish, which works fantastically with the belly pork. You could also add steamed or grilled leeks or roast cauliflower.

Serves 4–6

800g purple sprouting broccoli
200g black, red Russian or curly kale

For the mustard dressing:
1 garlic clove, crushed
2 teaspoons Dijon mustard
2 teaspoons honey
3 tablespoons good-quality red wine vinegar
100ml sunflower oil
sea salt and freshly ground black pepper
1 tablespoon mustard seeds

Steam the purple sprouting broccoli and kale over boiling water until just tender. Refresh in cold water, and drain. Whisk together all the ingredients for the dressing except the mustard seeds, and season to taste.

Dry-fry the mustard seeds until they're starting to pop, then add to the dressing.

Arrange the greens on a serving dish and drizzle over the mustard dressing.

Roast Pork Belly

Belly pork is a really flavoursome cut of meat. It needs to be cooked for a long time because of the amount of fat, but this will result in very tender meat and good crackling. It's important to score the skin – you can ask your butcher to do this for you – as it helps the crackling form.

Serves 6

sea salt
1–1.5kg piece of pork belly, scored
1 tablespoon olive oil
1 teaspoon crushed fennel seeds
2 onions, halved
1 carrot, roughly chopped
2 leeks, well washed and roughly chopped
500ml cider
500ml chicken stock
2 apples, peeled and finely chopped

Rub salt into the skin of the pork belly. Leave for about 1 hour. Meanwhile, preheat the oven to 220°C/Gas Mark 7.

Wipe away any moisture from the pork skin, rub with the oil and sprinkle with more salt and the crushed fennel seeds. Place the onions, carrot and leeks in a roasting tray.

Sit the pork belly on top of the vegetables and place in the hot oven for about 20 minutes. Then reduce the oven temperature to 140°C/Gas Mark 1 and cook for 3–3½ hours, or until tender. Remove to a warm place to rest.

Add 200ml boiling water to the roasting tin and scrape away any meat juices on the bottom. Push all the juices and the vegetables through a sieve into a pan. Add the cider and stock and reduce by about half, until starting to thicken. Add the chopped apples and simmer for another 10 minutes.

Serve with the sliced pork.

Kale Gratin

This recipe works well for most varieties of kale. If you're using cavolo nero, you definitely need to strip out the central stalk before you blanch the leaves, but if you're using smaller, less tough kale stems you may be able to get away with just removing the thickest bits of stalk. To strip the leaves from the stalk hold the thick end of the stem with one hand and wrap the other hand around the base of the leaves. Pull down and leaves should strip cleanly away from the stem.

Serves 4

4 bunches of kale, each about 150g
100g breadcrumbs
75g melting cheese, such as Gruyère or Fontina
1 tablespoon grated Parmesan cheese
50g unsalted butter
1 tablespoon extra virgin olive oil
1 onion, finely chopped
2 garlic cloves, crushed
1 dried chilli, stalk removed, deseeded if preferred, chopped
100ml double cream
sea salt and freshly ground black pepper

Preheat the oven to 200°C/Gas Mark 6.

Bring a large pan of water to the boil. Strip the green leaves from the stalks of the kale and discard the stems. Simmer the leaves in the boiling water for about 3 minutes. Drain well. Refresh in a bowl of very cold water, drain again and squeeze out any excess water.

In a bowl, combine the breadcrumbs and the two cheeses.

Place a pan over a medium heat and add the butter and oil. When heated, add the onion and fry for 3–4 minutes until transparent. Add the garlic and chilli and fry for another minute. Coarsely chop the kale and add to the pan. Cook for a couple of minutes, then add the cream. Mix well and season with salt and pepper. Remove from the heat and spoon the mixture into a gratin dish. Spread the breadcrumb mixture over the top and bake in the oven for about 20 minutes until golden brown.

Lime Cheesecake with Pineapple and Mango

A classic cheesecake adapted to incorporate some of our fairtrade imports. See Guy's video on our pineapple growers in Togo: www.riverford.co.uk/pineapples

Serves 10–12

For the base:
250g ginger biscuits
75g pecan nuts
1 tablespoon soft brown sugar
1 tablespoon stem ginger, chopped
75g unsalted butter, melted

For the filling:
3 eggs
200g caster sugar
420g cream cheese or mascarpone
½ teaspoon vanilla extract
zest and juice of 2 limes
1 tablespoon crème fraîche
1 tablespoon double cream
2 tablespoons desiccated coconut
sliced mango and pineapple, to serve

Preheat the oven to 170°C/Gas Mark 4. Line a 24cm springform tin with baking parchment.

Grind the biscuits, nuts, brown sugar and stem ginger in a food processor. Add the butter and mix well. Press into the base of the tin and bake for 10 minutes to set. Cool.

Reduce the oven temperature to 140°C/Gas Mark 1. Beat the eggs with the caster sugar until pale. In another bowl, mix the cream cheese with the vanilla and lime zest and juice. Whisk in the egg mix until well blended. Pour on to the crust and bake for about 50 minutes until set. Allow to cool.

Mix together the crème fraîche and cream and spread over the cheesecake. Toast the coconut in a dry frying pan until golden, then sprinkle this evenly on the top. Serve with the mango and pineapple.

Everyday

Broccoli with Wet Garlic
Calabrese Cooked in Red Wine
Bhaji Batter
Giorgio's Patatas Bravas
Salt Cod Fritters
Wild Garlic Mayo
Orecchiette with Purple Sprouting Broccoli
Wild Garlic Pesto
Spiced Chicken with Spring Greens
Spring Greens with Red Pepper
Spring Greens with Caraway and Lentils

Sunday

Pot-roast Veal Breast or Shoulder with Porcini,
Sage, Rosemary and Lemon
Mustard Mash
Spring Greens and Purple Sprouting Broccoli with Wild Garlic Pesto
Rhubarb and Praline Semifreddo

APRIL

Challenge and a little excitement

For the die-hard advocates of local food, April is the most challenging month of the year. The few remaining crops in the fields (swedes, leeks) are getting woody as they prepare to go to seed. The roots in store are sensing spring and sprouting as soon as they get warm. By the end of the month, our protestations about the 'hungry gap' and promises of good things to come are starting to sound lame. Our tunnels provide a little light relief with a few lettuces, salad leaves and spinach, but by the end of the month, in order to keep our customers happy in their kitchens, our growers in Spain and Italy or our farm in the French Vendée are providing up to 40 per cent of the box contents.

Deprivation and flavour

Over the years I have reached the conclusion that the slow growth that results from a little hardship is generally good for flavour but too much creates stunted bitterness – analogies to raising children? Spring greens have been bred to expect regular hits of ammonium nitrate through the winter from conventional (non-organic) growers. Nitrogen fertiliser is an organic no-no on account of its huge requirement for fossil fuels. Deprivation at the hands of an organic farmer can be good for the greens. If the wind is in the west in April, giving us growy, Devon dampness, the last organic greens arrive a month after the conventional crop (pumped up on ammonium nitrate) has finished and have a much superior flavour. In the occasional year when the wind is from the east – producing a cold, bright and dry April – they can rapidly become inedibly tough and bitter. If this happens, our appetite for greens is satisfied by the later varieties of purple sprouting broccoli – this splendid, rugged and flavoursome vegetable is one our customers never seem to tire of. By the end of the month we are on to picking the smaller secondary spears; they take for ever to pick but are often the best to eat. Tie them in bunches (a rubber band is fine) and stand upright in an inch of boiling water as you would asparagus to avoid overcooking the delicate florets. With determined picking they can still be cropping into May from a garden, but the growers in our co-op normally rebel at the fiddly task by the end of April and turn the sheep in.

Stealing from sheep

Most kales are long past their best, becoming tough and nasty as they put their final efforts into running to seed. We are normally happy to see the back of them, but after hard winters when greens can be in short supply,

we sometimes steal some 'thousand head' or 'hungry gap' kale from the cows and sheep. This traditional crop of the west of the country can throw a multitude of succulent shoots, each bearing a embryonic flower bud. For a brief period, before the flowers emerge, it can make very good eating.

Ransoms from the woods

From the deciduous woods we pick wild garlic, or ransoms, as it's known locally. In late February the dark green leaves emerge with tremendous vigour from bulbs, followed in April by a second wave germinating in a synchronous carpet from tiny black seeds in the leaf litter. It's a mad rush to develop leaves, trap enough light, flower, bear seed and stash away enough starch in a new bulb before the trees above burst into leaf and shade them out in early May. The pungent leaves can be eaten raw in salads, used in a gratin, made into a pesto or, my favourite, melted into a risotto. Picking ransoms started as a lucrative, if smelly, pocket-money earner for my children and their friends during the Easter holidays, but the crop has proved so popular with our customers that they have been unable to keep pace with demand.

Garlic is planted as single cloves in November and overwintered as a seedling. It gets going again in late February, and by late April resembles a small leek 10–20mm in diameter, starting to swell at the base as a new bulb is formed. In the early years we harvested it, fully formed and already starting to senesce, in late June, but in our climate we found it hard to get it consistently dry enough, quickly enough, for it to keep well. After seeing immature bulbs on sale as 'wet garlic' in an Andalucían market twenty years ago, we followed suit and have never looked back. I love it chopped straight into salads, stir-fries or risotto. It can be substituted for dry garlic (but use more and add it later in the cooking) but is probably at its best raw. Use the whole thing: bulb, stalk and even leaves, provided they are in good condition. Keep it in the fridge.

Rhubarb to the rescue

Indoor forced rhubarb is available from late January to March, the roots having been lifted from the fields in November or December and forced in warm dark sheds to produce a single etiolated crop of wonderfully tender stems, traditionally harvested by candlelight. Almost the entire forced crop comes from Yorkshire, where it has enjoyed a renaissance in recent years. Our rhubarb is grown and harvested outside as a perennial. After two years of establishment, while it builds up energy in its roots, we start picking the much stouter (and, I admit, slightly tougher) stems in late April, with the harvest running through to July, when they start to become tough and dry and we leave them to recharge their roots for next year. Outdoor rhubarb requires more cooking and a little more sugar than the forced crop but has the virtue of being much cheaper. Varieties vary in thickness of stalk, with the first, Timperley Early, generally having the thinnest, and the latest, Sutton's Seedless, the thickest. In my experience, the later, fatter varieties are just as good if not better. The best indication of quality is that the stalks are firm.

A plea for patience and seasonal realism

For the cook, April has all the excitement of spring but it is easy to feel impatient waiting for the arrival of new season crops. Cookery writers have a maddening tendency to tout vegetables a month ahead of there being any realistic chance of picking them, even in the mild south-west. The result is growers in perpetual pursuit of earlier harvests, which always come at a price in terms of the environment and quality. Quick-growing, early varieties, whether carrots, potatoes, purple sprouting or butternut squash, seldom have the best flavour. Pushing them on, whether with heat, crop covers, water or fertiliser, can result in substantial environmental impact. Be patient. Enjoy each vegetable as it arrives, at its best. Eat it in every way you can until you are thoroughly sick of it and happy to do without it until next year.

Quick and easy ideas
SPRING GREENS and
WET AND WILD GARLIC

Greens and garlic

Cook sliced wet garlic and shredded spring greens in olive oil for about 5 minutes or until the greens are wilted and tender. Finish with chopped wild garlic leaves and grated Parmesan cheese.

Stir-fried spring greens

Brown sesame seeds in sunflower oil, then add a little chopped chilli, garlic and ginger. Stir quickly and add shredded spring greens with a splash of soy sauce. Stir, cover and leave to wilt for 5 minutes.

Wet garlic spaghetti

Gently fry lots of chopped wet garlic in olive oil with fresh and dried chopped chilli. Toss with cooked spaghetti and chopped parsley.

Wet garlic and coconut dressing

Soak desiccated coconut in boiling water for 30 minutes. Squeeze out excess moisture and toast lightly in a medium oven until light brown. Mix with a little chopped wet garlic, cayenne, lime juice, fish sauce and sugar. Toss through cooked spring greens.

Wild garlic and eggs

Add shredded wild garlic leaves to eggs halfway through scrambling.

Wild garlic flowers

Use wild garlic flowers to decorate salads.

EVERYDAY

Broccoli with Wet Garlic

April is the start of the real hungry gap. During this time we start to import calabrese (broccoli) from Puglia in Italy. It comes from one of my favourite suppliers, Giancarlo Ceci, who also makes very good wine and olive oil. You could make this recipe with purple sprouting too. Wet garlic is completely different from dry garlic to cook with – it has a milder flavour and Guy claims he can eat it raw. It is very sweet but I think still too strong to eat without cooking. If wild garlic is around, then chop up some leaves and throw them in too.

Serves 4–6

500g broccoli
3 tablespoons olive oil
3 or 4 heads of 'wet' (new season's) garlic, chopped
sea salt and freshly ground black pepper
1 garlic clove, crushed
1 teaspoon caster sugar
150ml white wine
1 teaspoon thyme leaves
finely grated zest of ½ unwaxed lemon

Cut the broccoli into small florets, then peel the stem with a potato peeler and cut it into small batons.

Heat the oil in a large, wide, heavy-based pan, add the broccoli and chopped wet garlic and cook over a medium heat for about 5 minutes. Season well and, when the wet garlic starts to turn golden, add the crushed garlic, sugar and wine. Bring to a boil, add the thyme and lemon zest and reduce the heat. Cover and cook for 10 minutes, until the broccoli is tender. Check the seasoning and serve.

Calabrese Cooked in Red Wine

Another recipe for calabrese – this one is based on a dish by Marcella Hazan. You use red wine and rich, salty anchovies and olives to flavour the dish.

Serves 4–6

500g broccoli (calabrese)
175g onion, very thinly sliced
50g black olives, pitted and halved
4 anchovy fillets, roughly chopped
50g Parmesan cheese, pared into thin slivers
sea salt
4 tablespoons olive oil
175ml red wine

Cut the broccoli into small florets, then peel the stem with a potato peeler and cut it into small batons.

Layer up the ingredients in a shallow pan, starting with a thin layer of onions. Over this spread a layer of broccoli stalks. Dot with a few olives, a few anchovy pieces and a few slivers of Parmesan, seasoning sparingly with salt as you go. Drizzle a little olive oil over everything. Repeat the procedure with the stalks and onions, saving the broccoli florets for the top layer.

Add the wine, cover and cook over a low heat for 1 hour or until the wine has evaporated. The broccoli does have a dull-looking, limp appearance at this stage but it tastes very good.

Bhaji Batter

This is a really easy batter that you can use to deep-fry cauliflower, calabrese (broccoli) or even strips of roots. Fry the vegetables, dipped in batter, in a deep pan in about 3cm of hot sunflower oil, until the batter's just crisped.

Makes enough for 1kg vegetables

4 tablespoons gram flour
1 tablespoon rice flour
pinch of chilli powder, or to taste
1 tablespoon chopped coriander
100ml soda water

Sift the flours together, then stir in the chilli powder and coriander. Add the soda water gradually, stirring until the batter is the consistency of double cream.

Giorgio's Patatas Bravas

Giorgio owns the Old Bakery in Kingsbridge. He's from Greece and his restaurant specialises in tapas, mezze and sharing dishes. This is my son David's favourite – he calls them Giorgio's crispy potatoes, and can easily polish off a whole bowlful.

Serves 4–6

1kg potatoes (Giorgio particularly recommends Maris Piper or Peer)
3 teaspoons sweet paprika
sunflower oil, for deep-frying

For the sauce:
2 onions, finely chopped
1 tablespoon olive oil
sea salt and freshly ground black pepper
4 garlic cloves, chopped
400g tin chopped tomatoes
4 dried red chillies, stalks removed, deseeded if preferred
150ml extra virgin olive oil

To make the sauce, cook the onions over a medium heat in a small deep pan with the olive oil and a pinch of salt for about 10 minutes, until soft but not coloured. Add the garlic and cook for another minute. Tip in the tomatoes and chillies and simmer for half an hour. Season and blend, adding the extra virgin olive oil to make a smooth and glossy sauce.

Peel the potatoes and cut into 2cm dice. Cook in boiling salted water until just tender. Drain and shake to dry. Mix 2 teaspoons of salt with the paprika and toss the potatoes through this spice mix. Heat 2–3cm sunflower oil in a deep pan. Deep-fry the potatoes in batches (making sure you don't crowd the pan), until brown and crispy.

Reheat the tomato sauce and serve the potatoes and sauce separately.

Salt Cod Fritters

At 2010's Dartmouth Food Festival, I was one of the cookery demonstators promoting *The Devon Food Book*, a history of local food. I was surprised to learn that some of Dartmouth's wealth was founded on the salt cod industry, so this was one of the recipes we cooked. You could substitute cooked smoked haddock for the salt cod. We source good-quality, sustainable salt cod from Spanish food importers Brindisa. Serve with Wild Garlic Mayo (see opposite).

Serves 6

400g floury potatoes (baking potatoes are good)
300g cooked salt cod, flaked (see page 247)
1 bunch of spring onions, finely chopped
1 tablespoon chopped parsley
1 tablespoon chopped chives
sea salt and freshly ground black pepper
3 eggs
sunflower or mild olive oil, for deep-frying

Wash the potatoes and boil them in their skins until tender, then drain, peel and mash. Mix them with the cod, spring onions and herbs and season well. Add the eggs, one at a time, mixing well. Allow to cool.

Heat the oil in a deep pan or deep-fat fryer (check that the oil is hot by dropping in a piece of bread – if it sizzles and turns brown then the oil is ready).

Shape the cod mixture into egg-shaped cakes between two wet spoons, then drop them into the oil in batches, being sure not to crowd the pan, and cook until crisp and golden brown. Drain the excess fat on kitchen paper.

Wild Garlic Mayo

Makes about 200ml/Serves 10

100g wild garlic leaves
2 garlic cloves, crushed
3 egg yolks
juice of 1 lemon
1 teaspoon Dijon mustard
pinch of caster sugar
100ml sunflower oil
sea salt and freshly ground black pepper

Pour boiling water over the wild garlic leaves. Drain immediately, dry well and chop finely.

Place in a liquidiser with the garlic, egg yolks, lemon juice, mustard and sugar.

Start adding the sunflower oil from a jug very slowly to begin with, until the mixture emulsifies. Keep adding the oil in a slow drizzle until the mayo has thickened. Season well and chill until needed.

Orecchiette with Purple Sprouting Broccoli

At a food festival in Puglia, I was coaxed onto the stage in the town square by Mino, a local chef, to help him make fresh orecchiette. Having never done it before, I made a complete fool of myself, to the delight of the locals. Nevertheless, I've since found it to be a very absorbing and highly addictive pastime. This is a classic Pugliese dish using that particular type of pasta – but the dried form is fine unless you are into fresh pasta-making. Originally made with cime di rapa, it works well with purple sprouting broccoli instead.

Serves 4

4 garlic cloves, thinly sliced
2 dried chillies, stalks removed, deseeded if preferred, chopped
2 tablespoons olive oil, plus more to serve
8 anchovy fillets
sea salt and freshly ground black pepper
400g purple sprouting broccoli
350g orecchiette
grated Parmesan cheese, to serve

Cook the garlic and chillies in the olive oil in a large pan for a few minutes; don't let the garlic brown. Add the anchovies, remove the pan from the heat and stir vigorously so the anchovies 'melt' into the oil.

In a pan of boiling salted water, cook the purple sprouting broccoli – leaves and all – for about 4 minutes, until tender. Drain and roughly chop. Add to the anchovy oil and cook for about 5 minutes.

Meanwhile, cook the orecchiette for about 12 minutes (or according to the packet directions), until almost cooked but a little al dente. Drain well and place in the pan with the purple sprouting broccoli. Season well and add grated Parmesan to taste.

April

Wild Garlic Pesto

From Riverford Cook Anna Colquhoun, this recipe is a good standby for a quick pasta dish. It would also be good stuffed under chicken skin before roasting.

Makes about 250g

75g pine nuts
150g wild garlic leaves, washed and dried well
50g basil leaves
75g Parmesan cheese, finely grated
sea salt and freshly ground black pepper
extra virgin olive oil
lemon juice, to taste

Lightly toast the nuts in a dry frying pan.

Briefly blitz the leaves, cheese, nuts, a good pinch of salt and a few grinds of black pepper in a food processor, then continue to blend while pouring in oil through the spout. Stop when the mixture is a loose paste (you may need to scrape down the insides of the processor bowl once or twice as you go).

Finish with freshly squeezed lemon juice to taste – you'll probably need around a tablespoon – and check the seasoning.

Spiced Chicken with Spring Greens

This is a fresh, spicy dish to cook in one pot. There isn't much green stuff around at this time of year, but spring greens work really well in this. Serve with steamed rice.

Serves 4

4 chicken breasts, skinned
2 tablespoons sunflower oil
4 garlic cloves, crushed
4cm piece fresh root ginger, chopped
1 head of spring greens, washed and finely shredded
1 large bunch of coriander, finely chopped
1 dried chilli, stalk removed, deseeded if preferred, finely chopped
1 teaspoon ground cumin
1 teaspoon ground coriander
pinch of cayenne pepper
pinch of turmeric
1 teaspoon sea salt
juice of 1–2 lemons

In a large sauté pan or wok, brown the chicken breasts in the sunflower oil on both sides. Remove from the pan.

In a blender, make a paste with the garlic and ginger, adding a little water to help (you could use a pestle and mortar instead). Add to the same pan and stir-fry for about 2 minutes. Add all the other ingredients except the lemon juice and cook for 2 minutes.

Place the chicken breasts on top of the greens and pour in 100ml water. Bring to a simmer, then reduce the heat, cover and cook for 10 minutes.

Turn the chicken, cover again and cook for another 5 minutes, or until the chicken is tender. Add lemon juice to taste and serve.

Spring Greens with Red Pepper

Originally based on a Madhur Jaffrey recipe, this is a versatile red pepper paste. Joyce Molyneux used to cook chicken with something similar when I trained with her at the Carved Angel. Spring greens cooked like this are really good with other spiced vegetables or a curry, or could be served on their own with plain basmati rice.

Serves 6

1 red pepper, deseeded and chopped
½ red onion, chopped
2 garlic cloves, crushed
½ teaspoon blachan (shrimp paste) (optional)
1 red chilli, deseeded if preferred, chopped
pinch of cayenne pepper
2 tablespoons sunflower oil
4 heads of spring greens, washed and finely shredded
1 teaspoon caster sugar
juice of ½ lemon
sea salt and freshly ground black pepper

In a food processor or using a pestle and mortar, blend the pepper, onion, garlic, shrimp paste (if using), chilli and cayenne together with 100ml water to make a coarse paste.

Heat the oil in a deep, heavy-based pan over a high heat and cook the paste for 5 minutes, stirring continuously, until it is cooked (it will release its fragrance).

Add the spring greens and the rest of the ingredients with 100ml more water. Cover and cook slowly for 10 minutes or until the greens are tender.

April

Spring Greens with Caraway and Lentils

Caraway is often used with cabbage but here it's combined instead with spring greens. You need to use a bit extra to suit their strong flavour. This dish could be a simple meal on its own, or a great accompaniment to pork chops or sausages.

Serves 4–6

1½ tablespoons Puy lentils
2 garlic cloves, crushed, plus 1 whole
1 tablespoon olive oil, plus more for the lentils
sea salt and freshly ground black pepper
25g unsalted butter
2 teaspoons caraway seeds
2 heads of spring greens, washed and finely shredded
finely grated zest of 1 orange

Cover the Puy lentils with water in a saucepan, add the whole garlic clove, bring to a boil and simmer for 20 minutes. Drain, stir in enough oil to coat the lentils, and season while they're still hot.

Heat the 1 tablespoon of oil and the butter in a large saucepan and add the crushed garlic and the caraway seeds. When the seeds start to pop, add the spring greens and stir quickly both to combine and to stop the garlic burning.

Add the orange zest, reduce the heat, cover and cook for about 10 minutes. Add the lentils and mix well. Check the seasoning and serve.

SUNDAY

Pot-roast Veal Breast or Shoulder with Porcini, Sage, Rosemary and Lemon

We source our veal from Bocaddon Farm, in Cornwall. It is rose veal, a by-product of the dairy industry that's been raised as free-range, allowed to suckle and live in groups in the open air. It's a million miles from the caged lives of conventional veal calves. Veal isn't too expensive, particularly if you use the cheaper cuts such as shoulder or breast.

Serves 6

75g dried porcini
1–1.5kg rolled veal shoulder or breast
1 tablespoon olive oil
15g unsalted butter
4 garlic cloves, sliced
leaves from 1 bunch of sage
3 sprigs of rosemary
1 teaspoon fennel seeds
1 unwaxed lemon
1 litre hot chicken stock
100ml cream
sea salt and freshly ground black pepper

For the gremolata:
1 garlic clove, very finely chopped
2 tablespoons chopped parsley
finely grated zest of 1 unwaxed lemon

Soak the porcini in 500ml boiling water for 30 minutes. Sieve, reserving the soaking liquor, squeeze out excess liquid and chop finely.

Brown the veal joint in the olive oil and butter in a very large heavy-based saucepan or flameproof casserole, then remove and set aside. Reduce the heat and add the garlic, sage, rosemary and fennel seeds. Stir.

Remove the zest from the lemon with a vegetable peeler. Add to the pan. Stir in the chopped porcini and their reserved soaking liquor. Increase the heat, stir and reduce the liquid by cooking for 10 minutes. Add the stock and return the veal to the pan. Partially cover and cook over a low heat, turning the veal occasionally, for 2–3 hours.

When the meat is very tender, remove it to a warm place to rest. Increase the heat and reduce the sauce until it starts to thicken. Add the cream, return to a simmer and season.

Mix together all the ingredients for the gremolata.

Slice the veal to serve, topped with the sauce and sprinkled with a little of the gremolata.

Mustard Mash

The famous chef, Peter Gordon, in the early days of the Sugar Club in London, served the most delicious mustard mash and this is loosely based on his method. For best results, the potatoes need to be mashed or milled into the hot butter and everything beaten together while still warm. For variations, try adding chopped spring onions or some fresh buttered cabbage.

Serves 4–6

1kg floury potatoes, peeled and quartered
4 garlic cloves, peeled
100g unsalted butter
100ml double cream
2 teaspoons Dijon mustard
2 teaspoons wholegrain mustard
sea salt and freshly ground black pepper

Cover the potatoes and garlic with water and bring to a boil. Simmer for about 20 minutes. In another pan, heat the butter and cream with the mustards.

Drain the potatoes. Place a food mill (or mouli-légumes or potato ricer) over the butter mixture and use it to sieve the hot potatoes directly on to the hot mix. Beat well and season.

Spring Greens and Purple Sprouting Broccoli with Wild Garlic Pesto

At this time of year the shady lanes of Devon are full of the amazing smell of wild garlic. It's best to pick the green leaves when they're young, and you can also use the pretty white flowers in salads or for decoration on dishes. This recipe is simply a lovely combination of the few green things that are at their seasonal best.

Serves 4–6

200g purple sprouting broccoli
2 tablespoons olive oil
sea salt and freshly ground black pepper
2 heads of spring greens, washed and finely shredded
2 tablespoons Wild Garlic Pesto (see page 92)

Trim the purple sprouting broccoli, cutting off woody ends and slicing any thick pieces in half lengthways so all the pieces are roughly the same size.

Heat the oil in a pan, add the purple sprouting broccoli and fry quickly, stirring, until slightly browned. Season, pour in 100ml water, cover and cook for 5 minutes.

Add the spring greens to the pan, mix well and season, then cover and cook for 5 minutes more, or until all the vegetables are cooked.

Remove from the heat and either stir the pesto through or drizzle it over the top to serve.

Rhubarb and Praline Semifreddo

We served this on our first Italian night at the Field Kitchen. I think it's a perfect combination of two cultures – a classic Italian dish, made with the very English rhubarb. It's best to serve when just frozen.

Serves 6–8

For the praline:
75g flaked almonds
50g caster sugar

For the rhubarb:
500g rhubarb, cut into 1–2cm pieces
100g caster sugar
zest and juice of 1 orange
1 tablespoon grenadine (optional)

For the semifreddo:
4 eggs, separated
50g caster sugar
few drops of vanilla extract
500ml double cream
pinch of sea salt

To make the praline, in a non-stick frying pan, toast the almonds until lightly browned. Add the sugar, stirring continuously, and reduce the heat. Cook for 5 minutes, until the sugar has started to caramelise and the almonds are coated with the caramel. Scrape out on to a baking sheet and allow to cool. Then roughly smash with a rolling pin.

Cook the rhubarb slowly with the sugar, orange zest and juice and grenadine (if using), adding 100ml hot water, until just tender. Gently strain the cooking liquor, reserving the juice, cover and chill.

Beat the egg yolks for the semifreddo with the sugar and vanilla until pale and fluffy. Whip the cream separately until just holding soft peaks. Whip the egg whites separately to soft peaks. Fold the whites into the yolk mixture and gently combine with the cream. Fold in the smashed almonds and the rhubarb pieces and pour into a cling film-lined mould. Cover with more cling film. Place in a freezer for at least 5 hours, until set.

Serve with the reserved rhubarb juice.

Everyday

Asparagus, Egg, Prosciutto and Parmesan
Spinach and Coconut Soup
Salad of Grilled Asparagus, Goat's Cheese and Basil with Shaved Fennel
Spinach, Chickpeas and Toasted Almonds
Kedgeree with Spring Onions and Peas
Spinach and Lentil Soup with Sorrel
Triple Garlic Frittata
Mint and Onion Sauce for Lamb
Marsala Carrots

Sunday

Lamb Shoulder Stuffed with Apricots, Couscous, Hazelnuts and Mint
Roast Saffron Potatoes with Almonds and Bay
Grilled Asparagus with Orange and Olive Dressing
Rhubarb and Cinnamon Cake

MAY

Succulent leaves and sprouting roots

The first thing an emerging plant needs to do is to trap sunlight, so May is a leafy month, full of freshness and promise. But it still offers only limited culinary possibilities to a vegetable-loving, local-food enthusiast wanting some roots or fruits to go with their new season greens. May brings the very first outdoor lettuce (we favour the robust green Batavia, followed by the wonderfully sweet Little Gems) and the earliest sowing of salad leaves such as mustard, rocket and baby spinach. By the end of the month we might cut the first summer greens (spring-planted immature, loose-hearted cabbages) from our most favoured fields along the south Devon coast, but our veg boxes are all leaves with not much to accompany them. The last of the over-wintered cauliflower and purple sprouting can limp into May on colder sites but rapidly rising temperatures bring on the unstoppable urge to rush to seed for these crops. They have been in the ground since the previous July and even the most valiant efforts of plant breeders have not been able to suppress the urge to procreate as temperatures and day length increase.

Beware of local leeks in May. They will either have an inedible bolt in the middle like a tree trunk (which carries the nascent, starburst flower upwards) or have spent too long in cold store, in which case they will be yellow before you get them home.

Don't worry too much about sprouting potatoes. Provided they have been kept in the dark they can have a mat of sprouts and have gone quite soft but still eat well once the sprouts are removed. Keeping them in the fridge will help to keep sprouting under control. As the starch converts to sugar, ready to fuel sprouting, they can develop a pleasant sweetness at the end of the season. The increased sugars can result in an unsightly blackening when cooking (particularly chips), but they make great baked potatoes. Our favourite variety for the end of the season is the very sleepy and fairly flavoursome Valor, the very last to wake up and sense spring. It also has good resistance to blight, making it a favourite with Riverford's co-op members.

Some growers in Cornwall and along the south coast will already be harvesting new season early potatoes but, with a few notable exceptions (like the Jersey Royals, and I suspect even these are not what they used to be), these first liftings are of quick-growing, watery varieties pushed on with fertiliser and water, making them barely worth eating. The first of the flavoursome, slower-

growing varieties (Charlotte is our favourite) rarely reach any sensible size until early June.

Asparagus – a perennial challenge

Some welcome variation is provided by the perennials asparagus and rhubarb. Their well-established, giant root systems give them a head start on even the fastest annual that starts growing from seed. UK asparagus has a six-week season from early May to late June. It is one of the most difficult crops to grow organically because of the relentless battle with weeds; even an asparagus crop that has occupied the ground for ten years doesn't cast enough shade to suppress emerging weeds. I have yet to meet an organic grower who has made a profit from the crop, though many have tried. We keep trying because it is such an iconic announcement of summer. Knowing the effort that has gone into growing it, I urge you to be happy with spears of any size and shape, provided they are fresh. The fat ones may be more tender but the smaller ones have more taste. To extend the season a little and to keep the veg boxes interesting, we work with an inspiring grower near Granada, Pepe of Huertas Bajas, whose crop is enviably good. Asparagus is a crop to enjoy at every opportunity during its short season but to be avoided when it has to be flown from across the world. Although I'm pragmatic about importing some crops, I've always drawn the line at the environmental madness of air-freighting.

Vegetable New Year

May is the vegetable New Year – out with the old and in with the new. Some of the new is not quite ready and it is easy to be impatient for June, but there is already plenty for an imaginative and determined cook to choose from, especially if you love salads, simple greens, such as spinach, and asparagus. Spring growth, especially in organic farming where it has not been forced on with nitrogen, is the best you will see all year – relish it in its natural state. It's time to abandon the sauces and enjoy salads and naked, minimally cooked vegetables at their best. There's plenty more to come, so don't worry about overdoing it on asparagus; by the time you tire of it we will be into June with its rapidly broadening culinary horizons.

Quick and easy ideas
RHUBARB

Rhubarb compote

For compote, cook 500g rhubarb cut into thin sticks (about 4cm x 1cm) with 150g sugar, 150ml water, zest and juice of 2 oranges, 1 tablespoon grenadine and a thin slice of raw beetroot (a handy tip for a bit of extra colour – remember to remove before eating!). Cook slowly either in the oven or on the stove top until tender, about 15 minutes. Cool. Orange segments can be added to this to make rhubarb and orange compote.

Compote pudding

Put rhubarb compote in a dessert dish and top with whipped cream or syllabub. Sprinkle with crumbled gingernut biscuits and chopped hazelnuts and serve.

Rhubarb mess

Top meringue nests with whipped cream. Drizzle with custard and top with rhubarb compote. Serve like this, or mash it all up together to make rhubarb mess.

Rhubarb bellini

Blend and sieve rhubarb compote. Put a little in the bottom of a champagne flute and top with prosecco or other sparkling wine.

Rhubarb sauce

For rhubarb sauce, chop 3 sticks of rhubarb and cook with 2 tablespoons sugar and 150ml white wine until tender. Whisk in 25g butter. Serve, chunky or blended, with pork tenderloin or chops, or with mackerel. A little ginger can be added to the rhubarb.

EVERYDAY

Asparagus, Egg, Prosciutto and Parmesan

You could call this posh ham and eggs – with one of your five-a-day thrown in. It's a wonderful dish, similar to something I ate at E'cco in Brisbane, except there the egg part was an egg yolk ravioli. The timing of this dish is all-important – everything needs to be ready at the same time.

Serves 4

sea salt and freshly ground black pepper
4 eggs
1 bunch of asparagus
8 slices of prosciutto
50g Parmesan cheese, pared into slivers
extra virgin olive oil, to serve

Have two pans of simmering salted water ready, one shallow for the eggs, the other deeper for the asparagus. Break the eggs into the poaching pan, cover, leave for 1 minute, then turn off the heat.

At this point, add the asparagus to the deeper pan and simmer for 3 minutes. Drain and divide between 4 plates.

Place an egg on each plate of asparagus. Arrange the prosciutto on top and scatter with shaved Parmesan. (The easiest way to shave a chunk of cheese is with a potato peeler.)

Sprinkle with black pepper and salt and drizzle with extra virgin olive oil.

Spinach and Coconut Soup

Joyce Molyneux, my early mentor at the Carved Angel in Dartmouth, made a very simple spinach soup similar to this one – I've added spices and creamed coconut. The flavour of creamed coconut is much fuller than that of tinned coconut milk. You could use coconut milk in its place, however, just reduce the amount of stock to compensate for the extra liquid.

Serves 4

2 onions, finely chopped
2 tablespoons sunflower oil
2 garlic cloves, crushed
1 dried chilli, stalk removed, deseeded if preferred, chopped
pinch of ground cumin
400g spinach, washed and roughly chopped
1 litre hot chicken or vegetable stock
75g creamed coconut, grated
sea salt and freshly ground black pepper

Cook the onions in the sunflower oil in a large saucepan over a medium heat for 10 minutes until soft but not coloured. Add the garlic, chilli and cumin and cook for a few more minutes.

Add the spinach, stock and coconut. Cover and cook for 10 minutes.

Blend and check the seasoning.

Salad of Grilled Asparagus, Goat's Cheese and Basil with Shaved Fennel

In this recipe the goat's cheese is part of the dressing – a more interesting way of involving it in the salad than just crumbling it over. If the asparagus you're using is quite thick, you might need to pop it in the oven to finish off cooking.

Serves 4 as a starter

1 bunch of asparagus
2 tablespoons olive oil
sea salt and freshly ground black pepper
1 head of fennel
10 cherry tomatoes, slow-roasted (see page 195)
10 basil leaves, torn

For the dressing:
100g crumbly goat's cheese
50ml milk
juice of ½ lemon
1 teaspoon thyme leaves

Toss the asparagus in the oil, season, and grill on a hot griddle pan for a few minutes on each side. Set aside.

Trim the fennel, remove the core and shave finely on a mandolin or grater.

To make the dressing, crumble the goat's cheese into the milk, add the other ingredients, warm gently until melted together and season.

Place half the fennel in a serving dish, top with the asparagus and remaining fennel, scatter with the tomatoes, drizzle with the goat's cheese dressing, and finish with the basil.

Spinach, Chickpeas and Toasted Almonds

One of our former members of staff, Russell Goodwin, came up with this recipe, based on a dish he'd eaten in Spain. It would go well with the Sunday stuffed lamb shoulder (see page 123) or with the Chermoulah Chicken (see page 254) or is great just on its own.

Serves 2

1 red onion, finely chopped
1 tablespoon red wine vinegar
2 teaspoons brown sugar
1 tablespoon raisins
600g spinach or chard, thick stalks removed, washed
sea salt and freshly ground black pepper
150g cooked chickpeas (or tinned equivalent, well-rinsed)
2 tablespoons flaked almonds, toasted
pinch of cayenne pepper
2 tablespoons extra virgin olive oil

Start by soaking the red onion in the vinegar and sugar. At the same time, pour hot water over the raisins and leave both to soak for 30 minutes.

Cook the spinach or chard in boiling salted water for 3 minutes. Drain, refresh in cold water and squeeze out the excess water. Chop roughly and season.

Grind up half the chickpeas roughly in a food processor. Squeeze out the excess water from the raisins.

Take a large bowl and tip in the onion (with its sugar and vinegar), spinach or chard, whole and ground chickpeas, almonds and raisins and mix together.

Season well, and sprinkle with cayenne pepper and olive oil to serve.

Kedgeree with Spring Onions and Peas

I absolutely love smoked haddock and could eat kedgeree for breakfast every day. It's nice to freshen up the fish and rice with the spring onions and peas; in the traditional Indian version, these would have been lentils.

Serves 6

200g basmati rice
3 eggs
400g naturally smoked haddock
200ml milk
1 onion, finely chopped
15g unsalted butter
1 tablespoon sunflower oil
1 teaspoon cumin seeds
pinch of ground cinnamon
3 cardamom pods, crushed
1 teaspoon ground coriander
pinch of cayenne pepper
pinch of turmeric
1 bay leaf
2 garlic cloves, crushed
1 tablespoon desiccated coconut
sea salt and freshly ground black pepper
200g shelled peas or sliced sugar snap peas
handful of chopped coriander and parsley
1 bunch of spring onions, chopped

Soak the basmati rice in cold water for 15 minutes. Drain. Cook the eggs in boiling water for 6 minutes. Remove from the heat, drain and refresh in cold water. Peel and cut into quarters.

Poach the haddock in the milk for about 10 minutes until cooked (it will start to flake under the pressure of a fork), drain and reserve the cooking liquor. Peel the skin from the haddock and flake the flesh into large pieces.

Cook the onion in the butter and oil for 10 minutes, then add the spices, bay and garlic and cook for 1 minute. Add the drained rice and coconut and stir for a few minutes until well coated in the spices.

Make up the reserved haddock milk to 400ml with water and add to the rice with seasoning. When it has come to a boil, cover and simmer for 10 minutes. Fold in the peas, flaked haddock pieces and herbs. Allow to sit, still covered, for 5 minutes.

Serve topped with the quartered eggs and the spring onions.

Spinach and Lentil Soup with Sorrel

Sorrel leaves add so much to this soup – their distinctive lemony flavour makes it taste quite exceptional. Sorrel is easy to grow or forage for but if you can't get hold of any add more spinach and a little lemon juice.

Serves 4

1 onion, finely chopped
1 tablespoon olive oil
2 garlic cloves, crushed
400g spinach, well washed and roughly chopped
100g sorrel leaves, shredded
200g cooked Puy lentils
500ml chicken stock
sea salt and freshly ground black pepper
blob of crème fraîche
sprinkling of finely grated Parmesan cheese

Cook the onion in the oil in a large saucepan over a medium heat for 10 minutes until soft but not coloured. Add the garlic and cook for 1 minute, then increase the heat and add the spinach and sorrel leaves. Stir vigorously until wilted.

Add the lentils and stock, and bring to a simmer. Remove half the soup mix and blend, then return to the pan. Season.

Finish with a little crème fraîche and Parmesan.

Triple Garlic Frittata

This is a dish to make at the point in late spring when the wet and wild garlic seasons collide – the wild is on its way out and the wet is on its way in. If you can't get wild garlic, it also works well with shredded basil – stir this into the egg mixture before adding to the pan.

Serves 4

1 garlic clove, crushed
3–4 heads of wet garlic, chopped
2 tablespoons olive oil
1 small bunch of wild garlic leaves, washed and shredded
6 eggs
sea salt and freshly ground black pepper
1–2 handfuls of finely grated Parmesan cheese

Preheat the grill on its highest setting.

In a non-stick frying pan, cook the crushed garlic and chopped wet garlic in the oil for 3 minutes. Add the wild garlic and wilt the leaves for a minute.

Whisk the eggs in a bowl and season. Pour the egg mixture into the pan, lifting up the garlic to make sure the egg runs underneath. Cook over a low heat, continually running a palette knife around the edges to prevent sticking, and shaking the pan.

When the frittata is cooked on the bottom but still slightly runny on the top, sprinkle with Parmesan and flash under the hot grill until just set. Serve in slices with a little more Parmesan on top.

Mint and Onion Sauce for Lamb

The best thing to serve with spring season lamb is new young mint, which this simple sauce makes the best of.

Serves 6–8

4 white onions, finely chopped
75g unsalted butter
2 teaspoons plain flour
300ml milk
grated nutmeg
sea salt and freshly ground black pepper
2 tablespoons finely chopped mint

Cook the onions in the butter in a deep sauté pan very gently for about 20 minutes without browning. Stir in the flour and cook gently for about 3 minutes.

Heat up the milk and add gradually to the pan, whisking after each addition, until the sauce thickens. Season well with nutmeg, salt and pepper and simmer gently for 15 minutes. Add the mint and serve.

Marsala Carrots

Bunched young carrots will just be coming into season by the end of May and this is a great way to cook them, instead of just boiling them in water.

Serves 4–6

2 bunches of new carrots, trimmed
1 tablespoon olive oil
30g unsalted butter
sea salt and freshly ground black pepper
100ml Marsala (or 50ml dark rum and 50ml sherry)
1 tablespoon chopped parsley

Cut the carrots in half lengthways. Heat the oil and butter in a pan. When hot, add the carrots, season well, reduce the heat and cook for 5 minutes, stirring all the time. Add the Marsala, bring to a simmer, mix well, cover and leave to cook over a low heat for 10 minutes, until the carrots are tender.

Uncover and reduce any liquid left until it just forms a glaze for the carrots. Remove from the heat and sprinkle with parsley.

SUNDAY

Lamb Shoulder Stuffed with Apricots, Couscous, Hazelnuts and Mint

We often cook this dish at this time of year in the Field Kitchen. The distinctive, slightly Middle Eastern flavours liven up a meal at a time when the stronger-tasting summer veg is still around the corner. You can either pot-roast the lamb on top of the stove or cook slowly in a low oven.

Serves 6–8

1.2–1.5kg lamb shoulder, boned and rolled
sea salt and freshly ground black pepper
75g couscous
75g dried apricots, chopped
75g hazelnuts, toasted, skinned and chopped
2 garlic cloves, crushed
1 dried chilli, stalk removed, deseeded if preferred, finely chopped
1 tablespoon chopped mint
1½ tablespoons olive oil
250ml red wine
1 litre lamb or chicken stock

Preheat the oven to 140°C/Gas Mark 1.

Open up the lamb shoulder and season well.

In a bowl, mix the couscous with the apricots, hazelnuts, garlic, chilli, mint and ½ tablespoon olive oil, and season well. Press the mixture into the inside of the shoulder. Roll up again and fix securely.

Brown the lamb shoulder in the remaining oil in a large frying pan over a high heat. Place in an ovenproof dish in which it fits snugly. Deglaze the frying pan with wine and stock, bring to a boil and pour over the shoulder.

Slow-roast in the preheated oven for 3–4 hours or until the meat is tender. Remove the lamb from the juices and allow to rest in a warm place. Pour the juices into a pan and reduce by boiling rapidly to half the original volume. Carve the lamb and serve it with the sauce.

Roast Saffron Potatoes with Almonds and Bay

With even just a pinch of saffron in the water, the potatoes absorb its colour and flavour and the result is vibrant. Sometimes, later in the summer, we add roasted fennel to the dish, and waxy potatoes work well in it too.

Serves 4–6

1kg potatoes (still old, stored ones)
pinch of saffron
sea salt and freshly ground black pepper
1 tablespoon olive oil
1 tablespoon flaked almonds, chopped
4 bay leaves
4 sprigs of thyme
6 garlic cloves

Peel the potatoes and cut into quarters lengthways (or sixths if large). Place in a pan and just cover with water. Add the saffron and a good pinch of salt. Bring to a boil, simmer for 5 minutes, then remove from the heat. Leave the potatoes to soak in the saffron water for at least 1 hour.

Half an hour before serving, preheat the oven to 200°C/Gas Mark 6. Drain the potatoes and place in a bowl. Toss with the olive oil, almonds, herbs and garlic. Season well.

Place in a baking dish in the hot oven for 30 minutes until golden.

Grilled Asparagus with Orange and Olive Dressing

Based on a Chez Panisse recipe, this salad works well as a starter or a side dish. You can use spring onions instead of chives.

Serves 4 as a starter

1 bunch of asparagus
2 oranges
1 shallot, or ½ red onion, finely chopped
1 teaspoon soft brown sugar
1 teaspoon red wine vinegar
2 tablespoons good-quality extra virgin olive oil
sea salt and freshly ground black pepper
10 good-quality olives, stoned and finely chopped
1 tablespoon chopped chives

Prepare the asparagus by snapping off the tough woody ends. Finely grate the zest of the oranges into a bowl with the shallots.

Segment the oranges by slicing away the skin and pith and cutting out the segments. Set aside. Squeeze out the juice from the remaining orange flesh into the bowl with the shallots. Add the sugar and vinegar.

Toss the asparagus in a little olive oil and grill on a hot griddle pan for a couple of minutes each side (if the asparagus is thick, you may have to blanch it first for a few minutes or finish it in the oven).

Whisk the rest of the oil into the shallot dressing. Check the seasoning.

Drizzle the dressing over the warm asparagus and scatter with the orange segments, olives and chives.

Rhubarb and Cinnamon Cake

This is a cake, but with a moist 'puddingy' quality from the crème fraîche and the fruit in the batter. It is based on a recipe from Stephanie Alexander's *Cook's Companion*. Delicious served with poached rhubarb and fresh custard, with crème fraîche or simply on its own. It's a rhubarb recipe we make for the annual Real Food Festival in London, along with brown sugar meringues topped with cream, custard and poached rhubarb (see page 314 for meringue recipe).

Serves 10–12

60g unsalted butter, softened, plus more for the tin
380g soft brown sugar
3 large eggs
few drops of vanilla extract
pinch of salt
zest of 2 oranges
300g self-raising flour
1 teaspoon bicarbonate of soda
1 teaspoon ground cinnamon
250ml crème fraîche
450g rhubarb, cut into 1cm pieces

For the topping:
60g brown sugar
1 teaspoon ground cinnamon

Preheat the oven to 160°C/Gas Mark 3. Butter a 24cm springform cake tin and line with baking parchment.

Cream the butter and brown sugar together. Add the eggs, vanilla, salt and orange zest. Sift the flour, bicarbonate of soda and cinnamon into the mixture, and fold through the crème fraîche and rhubarb. Pour into the cake tin and sprinkle with the sugar and cinnamon for the topping.

Bake in the preheated oven for 40–50 minutes, until a skewer inserted in the centre comes out clean.

Everyday

Chicken Salad with an Elderflower and Tarragon Dressing
Duck with Turnips and Marmalade
Salad of Broad Beans, Feta and Mint
Gado Gado Sauce
Wild Rice, Spinach and Broad Bean Salad
Glazed Radishes
Spiced Turnips with Almonds and Coconut
New Potatoes with Crab, Chilli, Parsley and Lemon
Quick Turnips and Ham
Carrot and Kohlrabi Salad
Baked Ricotta with Gooseberry Compote
Cherry Clafoutis

Sunday

Confit of Salmon
Almond Aïoli
New Potato Salad with Red Onions and Broad Beans
Braised Little Gems, Radish, Spring Onions and Mint
White Chocolate Berry Cake

JUNE

The waiting is over

At last, the first pick of outdoor-grown strawberries announces that the months of deprivation are over. After twenty-five years of growing vegetables I am still excited by the first broad beans, gooseberries, courgettes, Charlotte potatoes, bunched carrots, summer bunched turnips ... June is so full of firsts, it is enough to make a vegetable-loving fifty-year-old almost childlike with excitement. I am not a diehard localist but June gives the payback that makes a little mild self-deprivation worthwhile – those strawberries would just not be the same if I had been eating Spanish Elsanta the week before.

Peas and first beans

I could happily eat broad beans followed by mounds of strawberries all month. The first broad beans of the year were sown in the autumn and flowered in April before many bees were about, often in patchy weather. Not surprisingly, pollination can be poor and as a result the first pods are often not well filled. By the end of the month we are into spring-sown varieties with well-packed pods that are more rewarding to shell. If you are a gardener, try picking out the leading shoots and quickly stir-frying. They can be wonderful if very fresh, but be careful only to use the very youngest three or four leaves or they will be tough and nasty. The first podding (or garden) peas are harvested at the beginning of the month, though we tend to concentrate on sugar snaps which are less tolerant of cold seedbeds and arrive a little later. It may sound heretical for Mr Riverford to say this, but frozen peas are very good and very cheap. There is a certain therapeutic value in podding fresh peas but the end result is only marginally better. As with beans, but tasting even better, the leading shoots of peas can be used in stir-fries or eaten raw in salads, they go very well with shavings of Parmesan.

Strawberries: what price reliable sweetness?

We often start the first strawberries, brought on by crop covers, at the end of May and by mid-June we're in the thick of them. Unlike most growers, we have stuck to growing strawberries outside, in the belief that – as with tomatoes – if we can cope with the uncertainty of the weather, the slower growth and full sun will produce better flavour. After some wet Junes resulting in the loss of much of the crop to botrytis, and annoying our customers by not delivering the strawberries they had ordered, we are considering following the herd. It is very difficult to run a business that is so susceptible to the vagaries of nature: the need for some consistency and predictability is a commercial reality. I just hope it is not the thin end of the wedge that will turn us into another Tesco.

We spend a lot of time agonising about strawberry and tomato varieties. The problem with flavour is that it is ultimately subjective. When we do blind taste trials with staff and customers, I am always disappointed by the way most people go for a simple balance of sweetness with acceptable acidity or sourness. Very few people will favour the deeper, more complex, aromatic flavours that characterise really exceptional fruit. The ubiquitous sweet and boring Elsanta strawberry is the result. It is annoyingly true of almost all managed human processes that those things that can be measured improve at the expense of those that aren't. Farming is no different, especially since the arrival of a simple and inexpensive tool called a brix monitor, which measures sugar levels. The pressure on breeders and growers is thus to produce ever sweeter fruit and even vegetables at the cost of other flavours – and, I suspect, nutritional value, which has been declining markedly since the 1970s.

Keep it simple

June is still a leafy month, with a predominance of spinach, cabbage and lettuces, but we also see the first flowers (broccoli), fruits (courgettes and perhaps the very first tomatoes), tubers (potatoes), roots (carrots, beets, turnips and kohlrabi) and pods (peas and broad beans), which collectively bring back welcome variety and balance. Our veg boxes tend to look excellent, with produce grown in plenty of light and a steady but not excessive release of fertility from a warming soil. This is the month to keep your cooking simple and light: these new season vegetables need very little cooking and no sauces. I even find myself getting irritable when my family put butter on them; it seems almost disrespectful to their perfection. A man obsessed? In June perhaps.

Quick and easy ideas
BROAD BEANS

Young broad beans raw

When very young, broad beans can be podded and eaten raw. Serve with pecorino and olive oil.

Young broad bean pods

When young, broad beans can also be cooked and eaten in their pods. Top and tail young beans. Chop into 1cm lengths and cook with chopped onion, garlic, parsley and ham in a little oil until almost tender. Add a little water and sherry, cover and cook until tender.

Broad bean purée

Blanch new season young broad beans (boil for 2 minutes then refresh in cold water), then purée or mash with crushed garlic, shredded fresh mint, grated pecorino and extra virgin olive oil. Spread on bruschetta.

Broad beans with Puy lentils

To make broad beans go further add a few tablespoons of cooked Puy lentils to blanched broad beans along with crushed garlic and shredded mint. Drizzle with extra virgin olive oil.

Fresh broad beans and artichoke hearts

Combine 150g cooked broad beans with 4 cooked artichoke hearts cut into wedges, 4 sliced spring onions, 1 tablespoon chopped preserved lemon (or use the zest of 1 lemon), a pinch of sumac, olive oil and chopped dill. Season well, toss together and serve with grilled fish.

EVERYDAY

Chicken Salad with an Elderflower and Tarragon Dressing

This is based on a Joyce Molyneux recipe from the Carved Angel. Joyce used elderflower vinegar, which she'd made the year before by steeping elder-flowers in white wine vinegar. I've adapted the recipe to use cordial in place of the vinegar.

Serves 4–6 as a starter

2 chicken breasts, skinned
about 300ml chicken stock
½ canteloupe or honeydew melon
2 small avocados
juice of ½ lemon
1 bunch of watercress, washed

For the dressing:
1½ tablespoons tarragon vinegar or white wine vinegar
1 teaspoon elderflower cordial
80ml groundnut oil
70ml single cream
2 teaspoons finely chopped tarragon
sea salt and freshly ground black pepper

Poach the chicken breasts gently in the stock for about 15 minutes, or until just cooked (they will feel firm). Leave in the stock for 10 minutes, then remove and allow to cool. Cut the cold chicken into roughly 2cm pieces. Reserve the stock for another use.

Cut the melon and avocado flesh into chunks about the same size. Squeeze a little lemon over the avocado.

In a liquidiser, blend all the dressing ingredients together until they emulsify (or whisk by hand, but you'll get the best results with a liquidiser). Gently mix the chicken, melon and avocado in a bowl with 2 tablespoons of the dressing. Arrange on a plate with the watercress and drizzle more dressing over.

Duck with Turnips and Marmalade

The new turnips available in June are small and sweet. Mixed with the classic combination of duck and orange, they make a stunning dish. Everything is cooked in one pan and the turnips cooked in duck fat are particularly good. At the Field Kitchen, our duck comes from Dan the duck man, based at Sladesdown Farm, Landscove, about a mile up the road.

Serves 4

3 duck breasts
4 large or 8 small turnips, peeled if necessary and cut into wedges
2 tablespoons marmalade
2 teaspoons balsamic vinegar
sea salt and freshly ground black pepper
25g unsalted butter
1 tablespoon chopped parsley

Preheat the oven to 200°C/Gas Mark 6.

Place the duck breasts skin-side down in a very hot, large, ovenproof, preferably non-stick frying pan. Reduce the heat a little and cook for about 5 minutes before turning over to brown the other side.

At this point, add the turnips and start to cook them in the duck fat. After about 3 minutes, place the whole pan in the hot oven for 8 minutes. Take out of the oven and remove the duck to a warmed plate to rest. Pour off excess duck fat (it can be used for roast potatoes).

Add the marmalade and vinegar to the pan, pour in 150ml water and cook over a high heat until the turnips are tender. Remove from the heat. Season the sauce and stir in the butter.

Slice the duck and place on a warmed serving dish. Add the turnips, pour over the sauce and sprinkle with parsley.

Salad of Broad Beans, Feta and Mint

A lovely salad to make with the first broad beans of the year – they shouldn't need anything more than shelling, but peel any that have thick skins.

Serves 4

300g broad beans, shelled weight
50g feta cheese
1 tablespoon chopped mint
1 tablespoon extra virgin olive oil
juice of ½ lemon
sea salt and freshly ground black pepper

Blanch the broad beans in boiling water for 2–3 minutes, then refresh in cold water and drain. Peel any large beans with tough skins. Place in a bowl, crumble the feta over and sprinkle with the mint. Dress with the olive oil, lemon juice, salt and pepper.

Gado Gado Sauce

Gado gado is an Indonesian peanut sauce that is great with most vegetables, either raw or cooked – I would use anything from blanched purple sprouting broccoli, cauliflower, French beans or cabbage to raw carrot, kohlrabi, cucumber or beansprouts.

Makes enough for 1kg vegetables

1 small red onion, finely chopped
1 garlic clove, crushed
1 red chilli, deseeded if preferred, chopped
1 tablespoon sunflower oil
1 teaspoon ground chilli
1 tablespoon palm or soft brown sugar
1 teaspoon tamarind paste
1 teaspoon thick soy sauce (kecap manis), or 1 teaspoon dark soy sauce
    mixed with 2 teaspoons brown sugar
250ml coconut milk
100g salted peanuts, ground fine but not to a paste
1 teaspoon fish sauce, or to taste

Cook the onion, garlic and red chilli in the oil for 5 minutes until soft. Add the ground chilli, sugar, tamarind, soy and coconut milk and bring to a boil. Tip in the peanuts and simmer for 5 minutes; the sauce should thicken. Finish with fish sauce to taste.

Wild Rice, Spinach and Broad Bean Salad

This is another of Riverford Cook Francesca Melman's recipes. What makes it distinctive is using the oil that the onions have been cooked in for the dressing. The sweet onions are freshened by the sharpness of the pomegranate molasses. This is available from Middle Eastern and health food shops.

Serves 4–6

125g wild rice
sea salt and freshly ground black pepper
2 onions, thinly sliced
4 tablespoons olive oil
200g broad beans, shelled weight
2 tablespoons pomegranate molasses
100g young spinach leaves

Cook the wild rice in boiling salted water for 30–40 minutes, until tender. Drain and allow to cool.

Cook the onions in the olive oil for 20–30 minutes, until soft and slightly caramelised. Drain and reserve the cooking oil.

Blanch the broad beans in boiling salted water for 3 minutes. Drain. Peel any large beans with tough skins.

Add the pomegranate molasses to the onion cooking oil and mix well. Season with salt and pepper.

Put all the ingredients in a large bowl, season and toss with the molasses dressing. Serve.

Glazed Radishes

Cooked radishes are quite unusual – I once ate them cooked by Nigel Marriage with coconut rice and sweetbreads at Effings in Totnes. This version makes a great side dish with grilled lamb or the Chermoulah Chicken (see page 254).

Serves 4

20 radishes, trimmed and halved
25g unsalted butter
1 tablespoon brown sugar
1 tablespoon balsamic vinegar
sea salt and freshly ground black pepper
chopped mint, to serve

Mix the radishes in a pan with all the other ingredients except the mint. Add 100ml water and bring to a simmer, then boil over a high heat for 5 minutes, stirring continuously.

Reduce the heat and cook for another 5 minutes, until the radishes are tender and glazed.

Season well and sprinkle with mint.

Spiced Turnips with Almonds and Coconut

There are a lot of turnip-haters out there – perhaps this delicately spiced dish will change their minds.

Serves 4

2 tablespoons flaked almonds
2 tablespoons desiccated coconut
1 tablespoon poppy seeds
1 tablespoon sesame seeds
2 teaspoons coriander seeds
200ml plain yoghurt
2 onions, finely chopped
2 tablespoons sunflower oil
2 garlic cloves, crushed
2cm piece fresh root ginger, grated
2 chillies, deseeded if preferred, chopped
1kg turnips, cut into 2cm dice
sea salt and cayenne pepper, to taste

Dry-fry the almonds and coconut with all the seeds in a small frying pan until lightly browned. Cool and grind to a fine paste in a mortar or spice mill. Mix with the yoghurt.

Cook the onions in the oil in a large, heavy-based pan for 10 minutes without browning, then add the garlic, ginger and chillies. Increase the heat, add the turnips and stir vigorously.

Add the spiced yoghurt and cook for 5 minutes, stirring well to prevent sticking. Add 150ml water, bring to a simmer, cover and cook for 15 minutes (adding more water if required), until the turnips are tender. Season well with salt and cayenne pepper.

New Potatoes with Crab, Chilli, Parsley and Lemon

We devised this recipe for the South Devon 'Cracking Crab' celebration. I'd normally use the dressing as a sauce for spaghetti, or on bruschetta with some shaved fennel, but I think it works well with new potatoes too.

Serves 4

1kg new potatoes
sea salt and freshly ground black pepper
150g picked white crab meat
juice of 1 lemon, plus more if needed
1 garlic clove, crushed
1 red chilli, deseeded if preferred, chopped
2 tablespoons chopped parsley
3 tablespoons extra virgin olive oil

Cook the potatoes in boiling salted water for 15–20 minutes, then drain. Allow to cool, then cut them into halves or quarters.

Mix the rest of the ingredients together and toss through the potatoes.

Adjust the seasoning and add extra lemon juice if required.

Quick Turnips and Ham

Turnips and ham is quite a classic combination, and I think best at this time of year when the turnips are young, small and sweet. Use good-quality, meaty ham.

Serves 4

4–6 turnips, peeled if necessary and cut into 1–2cm chunks
sea salt and freshly ground black pepper
250g thickly sliced ham, cut into cubes
15g unsalted butter
2 teaspoons brown sugar
1 tablespoon chopped parsley
splash of sherry vinegar

Blanch the turnips in boiling salted water for 5 minutes. Drain.

In a large pan, brown the ham in the butter, then add the blanched turnips and sprinkle with the sugar. Increase the heat and cook for a minute, then cover and reduce the heat once more. Cook slowly until the turnips are tender. Sprinkle with parsley and vinegar, season and add a splash more sherry vinegar to serve.

Carrot and Kohlrabi Salad

Kohlrabi can be very good eaten raw – in fact, this is how some people prefer it. It goes well with the Asian flavours in this recipe.

Serves 4–6

1 kohlrabi, peeled and grated
3 large carrots, grated
2 garlic cloves, crushed
1 red chilli, deseeded if preferred, finely chopped
2cm piece fresh root ginger, finely grated
1 teaspoon brown sugar
zest of 1 unwaxed lemon
juice of 2 limes
2 teaspoons fish sauce
2 tablespoons chopped coriander
2 tablespoons peanuts, roasted and chopped

Mix all the ingredients together.

Baked Ricotta with Gooseberry Compote

This simple baked ricotta recipe is from 'Posh' Ben Bulger in the Field Kitchen. Serve it with stewed rhubarb or berries at other times of the year.

Serves 4

400g ricotta
120g honey
3 eggs, separated
few drops of vanilla extract
unsalted butter, for the dish
icing sugar, for dusting the dish

For the compote:
300g gooseberries, topped and tailed
1 elderflower head (or a splash of elderflower cordial)
2 tablespoons caster sugar, plus more if needed
30g unsalted butter

Put all the ingredients for the compote in a pan and cook over a low heat until the gooseberries start to split. Check the sweetness, adjust if necessary and allow to cool. Remove the elderflower (if using). Preheat the oven to 170°C/ Gas Mark 4.

In a food processor, mix the ricotta, honey and egg yolks with the vanilla. Whisk the egg whites until stiff and fold into the ricotta.

Butter an ovenproof dish and dust with icing sugar before adding the ricotta mixture. Bake for 20 minutes until golden. Serve with the fruit compote.

Cherry Clafoutis

This is a fabulous pudding – the batter is delicious, and you can add a tablespoon of kirsch to it to make it alcoholic if you like. For a brief period, you can get good British cherries, but you do otherwise have to use imported ones. Stoning the cherries can take a bit of time – it is much quicker if you have a cherry stoner. This is a gluten-free recipe.

Serves 6–8

For the cherries:
50g unsalted butter
900g cherries, stoned
100g caster sugar
pinch of ground cinnamon
finely grated zest and juice of 1 orange

For the batter:
4 eggs, separated
200g caster sugar
125g ground almonds
1 tablespoon rice flour
1 teaspoon vanilla extract
½ teaspoon almond extract
250ml crème fraîche
pinch of salt
icing sugar, for dusting

Preheat the oven to 190°C/Gas Mark 5.

Melt the butter in a frying pan until foaming. Add the cherries, sugar, cinnamon and orange zest and juice. Cook for 10 minutes until the cherries are tender and the juices thickened. Pour into a shallow ovenproof pudding dish.

Beat the egg yolks with the caster sugar until light and creamy. Mix in the almonds, rice flour, vanilla and almond extracts and crème fraîche. In another bowl, beat the egg whites with the salt until soft peaks form, then fold them into the batter. Pour the batter over the fruit and bake in the hot oven for about 25 minutes, until set. Dust with icing sugar and serve immediately or at room temperature.

Confit of Salmon

An interesting way of cooking salmon – you cure it slightly in the sugar and salt, then bake it very slowly in oil. Serve with Almond Aïoli (see opposite). You could just grill the salmon if you prefer, it will still be delicious with the aïoli.

Serves 4

80g brown sugar
30g sea salt
500g piece of salmon, or 4 x 120g pieces
150ml rapeseed or olive oil
bouquet garni of fennel, bay and thyme
4 garlic cloves

Preheat the oven to 130°C/Gas Mark 1. Rub the brown sugar and salt over the salmon. Leave for about 1 hour. Wipe off the excess salt and sugar. Using a baking dish in which the salmon piece or pieces will fit snugly, add the oil, herbs and garlic and allow to warm up in the preheated oven for 10 minutes. Place the salmon carefully in the oil and cook in the oven, uncovered, for 10–12 minutes or until the salmon is just done. Remove from the oil and serve with almond aïoli.

Almond Aïoli

I like the flavour that toasted almonds add to a traditional aïoli. It's really good with salt cod, with raw vegetables, such as celery, fennel, radishes, cucumber or kohlrabi, or with poached chicken.

Makes plenty to serve 4 with the Confit of Salmon (see opposite)

50g flaked almonds
2 garlic cloves, crushed
2 egg yolks
juice of 1 lemon
300ml sunflower oil
100ml olive oil
sea salt and freshly ground black pepper

Toast the almonds in a pan until light brown in colour. Chop roughly and set aside.

Mix the garlic, egg yolks and lemon juice together in a bowl (or in a food processor or liquidiser). Very slowly add the oils in a thin, steady stream until the mixture has emulsified and thickened. Stir in the chopped almonds and season.

New Potato Salad with Red Onions and Broad Beans

To have this salad at its best, add the potatoes to the vinegar reduction while they're still warm and season well. At this time of year, it's fine to keep the broad beans in their skins.

Serves 4–6

1kg new potatoes, washed
sea salt and freshly ground black pepper
2 red onions, finely chopped
4 tablespoons olive oil
2 garlic cloves, crushed
4 tablespoons white wine vinegar
1 tablespoon caster sugar
200g broad beans, shelled weight
1 tablespoon chopped chives, mint or parsley

Cook the new potatoes in boiling salted water for 15 minutes or until just cooked. Cook the onions slowly in half the olive oil for 10 minutes until soft but not brown. Add the garlic, vinegar and sugar and mix well. Reduce the liquid by boiling until only 2 tablespoons remain.

Quarter or halve the new potatoes and toss in the reduced liquid while still warm. Season well and stir in the remaining oil. Cover and keep warm.

Cook the broad beans in boiling salted water for 3–4 minutes until tender. Drain and gently combine with the potatoes and herbs.

Braised Little Gems, Radish, Spring Onions and Mint

You don't have to eat lettuce raw – it is also very good cooked. This salad is a versatile summer side dish.

Serves 4–6

2 tablespoons olive oil
3 Little Gem lettuces, cut into eighths lengthways
2 garlic cloves, crushed
1 teaspoon caster sugar
1 teaspoon cider vinegar
sea salt and freshly ground black pepper
10 radishes, cut into very thin rounds
1 bunch of spring onions, finely chopped
leaves from 1 bunch of mint, shredded

Heat the oil in a large, heavy-based pan. Add the Little Gem wedges and stir quickly, then add the garlic, sugar and vinegar and stir for about 10 minutes until wilted. Season well.

Remove from the heat and add the rest of the ingredients, reserving some to sprinkle on the top when serving.

White Chocolate Berry Cake

June is when many people's favourite fruit – the strawberry – comes into its own. In this gooey cake you can use strawberries and a selection of other seasonal berries to create a wonderful pudding – almost like a white tiramisu. For the other berries try tayberries, redcurrants, blackcurrants or cherries.

Serves 10

For the sponge:
unsalted butter, for the tins
4 eggs
100g caster sugar
drop of almond extract
100g plain flour, sifted

For the cream filling:
200g white chocolate, chopped
150ml plus 2 tablespoons double cream
few drops of vanilla extract
250g tub mascarpone
finely grated zest and juice of 1 orange
1 sheet gelatine

For the berry filling:
100g caster sugar
200g raspberries, blackcurrants or redcurrants
2 tablespoons crème de framboise or brandy
200g other mixed berries, including strawberries

To finish:
25–30g dark chocolate
handful of mixed berries

Preheat the oven to 160°C/Gas Mark 3. Butter two 24cm cake tins and line with baking parchment.

Whisk the eggs with the sugar and almond extract until pale and doubled in volume. Fold in the flour and divide the batter between the cake tins. Bake in the preheated oven for 20 minutes until firm. Allow to cool.

To make the cream filling, melt the white chocolate with 2 tablespoons of the double cream and the vanilla in a bowl over a pan of very hot water (make sure the base of the bowl does not touch the water).

Whip together the mascarpone, remaining double cream and the orange zest and juice.

Soak the gelatine in a bowl of cold water. When it's squidgy, squeeze out the water, add the gelatine to the white chocolate and mix well. Allow to cool completely. Fold in the mascarpone cream and set aside.

For the berry filling, place the caster sugar in a saucepan with 100ml water and heat gently until the sugar dissolves, then increase the heat and simmer for 5 minutes. Add the raspberries, blackcurrants or redcurrants and simmer for a further 5 minutes. Cool a little, then add the raspberry liqueur or brandy. Divide the raspberry mixture in two and use half to soak each sponge (the soggier the better!).

Place one sponge on a serving dish and spread with some of the mascarpone-white chocolate cream. Top with the sliced strawberries and other berries if using. Place the other sponge on top and spread with the remaining cream, spreading it gently around the sides of the cake too. If possible, place in the fridge for 30 minutes. Before serving, grate dark chocolate over the top and garnish with the odd berry.

Everyday

Carrot Fritters
Summer Minestrone with Chicken and Herbs
Beetroot, Smoked Trout and Toasted Buckwheat
Courgette Fritters with Cheese
Courgette Fritters
Stuffed Courgette Flowers
Beetroot Tzatziki
Pork Larp
Sugar Snap Peas and French Beans with Tahini Dressing
Salmon and Soba Noodles
Grilled Lamb and Sugar Snap Salad
Vietnamese Spring Rolls and Nuoc Cham Dipping Sauce
Bean and Fennel Salad
John Dory as in Sicily
Blackcurrant Mess

Sunday

Lamb Cooked in Milk with Fennel
Hispi Cabbage, Summer Greens, Broad Beans and Lentils
Artichoke Gratin
Apricot Brioche Pudding

JULY

Hectic abundance

July is the busiest month of the year for us in the fields. For our veg box cooks it marks the start of four months of ever-increasing abundance and variety. As the season progresses and plant physiology develops, more flowers, fruits and pods are added to the leaves that dominated in May and June. If we discount produce from heated greenhouses, with their insane use of fossil fuels, early July is the start of the season for tomatoes and cucumbers, with peppers and the first chillies and aubergines arriving by the end of the month.

Outside, the early broad beans start getting tough and by the end of the month have had their day. We could continue with later sowings but black fly becomes more of a problem. As French beans come into season outside at the end of the month, most people have had enough of podding broad beans so we move on. If your remaining broad beans look large (much more than 20mm) and tough (a good indication is a darkening of the seed stem attaching them to the pod), then they can be blanched and slipped out of their skins – not something to do if feeling harassed and in need of a quick meal, but a satisfying task if you have the time and there is something interesting on the radio. Our courgettes are starting to come through and will be the staple of many summer suppers over the next couple of months.

A succession of fruit

The 'natural' strawberry season is over by mid July in Devon and it is time to move on to raspberries, currants and the first of the plums. Such a short season is unacceptable to supermarkets so, through various clever techniques like planting out runners from cold stores and early deflowering of ever-bearing varieties, their strawberry season continues right into October, with a progressive decline in flavour and increase in price.

Planting for autumn and winter

As the days start to shorten, plantings concertina; in March we plant every three weeks to get one week between harvests in May or June. In July we plant every three days, creating a hectic crescendo. It becomes crucial to get our planting dates right. In terms of the growth of, say, a cabbage, a day in July is worth two weeks in December and a month in January, so even a short delay can mean gaping winter shortages in veg box content. For each crop there comes a date – July 20 for leeks, August 7 for most lettuce, August 4 for cauliflower – when there is not enough growth left in the year to take the crop to maturity and the planting season is over.

A cook's delight

July is an exciting month for cooks with new crops coming into season every week. There is still the excitement of the first raspberry, chilli or tomato, but with the growing abundance I feel less precious about appreciating them in their natural state and instead enjoy the return of more indulgent dishes like gratins and fritters. With long days, warm nights and an active soil producing luxuriant growth, inexperienced gardeners may start to feel overwhelmed by even a small vegetable patch and wish they had spaced out those spring plantings. Prices should be starting to fall as we move into the main season, with yields increasing and growers' costs falling. The flavour of potatoes improves as slower-maturing varieties come to market. Summer beets, carrots and turnips are at their best – wonderfully tender and bursting with flavour. French beans, fennel, artichokes, celery and more come into season to join the abundance of salads and leaves. With raspberries and currants cropping, we are in the middle of the succession of summer berries, which we complement with the occasional melon from our farm in France, making July a wonderful month for puddings.

Quick and easy ideas
GLOBE ARTICHOKES

Artichoke and spinach gratin

Boil artichokes for 15 minutes or until the outer leaves pull away easily. Cool, then trim back the tough leaves and remove the hairy choke. Slice the hearts. Steam 200g spinach, squeeze out excess moisture and chop roughly. Mix with the artichoke slices in a shallow, ovenproof dish. Season. Top with 200ml béchamel sauce. Sprinkle with breadcrumbs and cheese and bake for 20 minutes at 200°C/Gas Mark 6.

Warm artichoke dip

Roughly chop cooked artichoke hearts with a little crushed garlic, mayonnaise and grated Parmesan cheese. Blend to a coarse mixture. Add chopped chilli and a sprinkling of paprika. Transfer to an ovenproof dish and bake in a medium oven for 15 minutes. Serve hot with crusty bread or tortilla chips.

Artichoke hearts with potatoes and peas

Toss wedges of cooked artichoke hearts with cooked new potatoes and peas. Dress with oil and lemon. Season and serve.

Dressed young artichokes

Prepare young artichokes quickly (trimming tough outer leaves) and rub with lemon to stop them browning. Cut into slices and dress with olive oil and lemon. Season. Serve with bresaola or cured pork.

Deep-fried artichokes

Small, young artichokes can be deep-fried whole. Trim and open up the leaves with your fingers. Deep-fry in hot oil for about 6–7 minutes until golden. Sprinkle with salt and vinegar.

EVERYDAY

Carrot Fritters

Simply deep-frying the new season carrots with spices, so they are just cooked, is the perfect way to show off their flavour. A lovely snack to have with drinks, or a side dish for an Asian-inspired meal.

Serves 4

1 teaspoon ground cumin
1 teaspoon ground coriander
pinch of turmeric
pinch of cayenne pepper
100g gram flour
50g plain flour
1 teaspoon sea salt
125ml lager or pale ale
1 large egg, beaten
200g carrot, grated
1 bunch of spring onions, finely chopped
1 tablespoon chopped mint
oil, for deep-frying

Sift the spices, flours and salt into a bowl. Whisk in the beer and egg to make a thick batter. Mix in the carrot, spring onions and mint.

Heat 2–3cm oil in a deep pan, until hot (drop a piece of bread in to test – if it sizzles and turns brown then the oil is ready). Shape portions of the fritter batter between 2 teaspoons and drop them into the oil. Be careful not to crowd the pan, or the temperature will drop and the fritters will be soggy. Deep-fry, turning once, until golden brown all over. Drain on kitchen paper. Serve.

Summer Minestrone with Chicken and Herbs

This summery dish is a take on Provençal pistou soup. You don't need to follow the recipe exactly. There are so many lovely vegetables available in July, just use whatever is fresh and to hand. But it is vital to use very good stock, preferably home-made chicken stock (see page xviii).

Serves 6

1 onion, finely chopped
1 celery stick, finely chopped
1 carrot, finely chopped
1 tablespoon olive oil
1 sprig of thyme
sea salt and freshly ground black pepper
3 garlic cloves, crushed
4 tomatoes, peeled and chopped
150g French beans, cut into 1cm pieces
150g trimmed runner beans, cut into 1cm pieces
2 courgettes, finely chopped
1 litre hot chicken stock
75g orzo pasta
150g broad beans, shelled weight
150g spinach leaves, shredded
400g tin white beans, drained and rinsed
2 chicken breasts, cooked and shredded
extra virgin olive oil, to serve
2 tablespoons summer herbs, such as basil, tarragon, chives or chervil

In a large soup pan, cook the onion, celery and carrot in the olive oil with the thyme and a little salt for 10 minutes, until soft but not coloured. Add the garlic and cook for another minute, then add the tomatoes, French and runner beans, and the courgettes. Cook well together, and season.

Pour in the stock and pasta and simmer for 10 minutes, or until the orzo is al dente. Now add the broad beans and spinach and cook for a couple of minutes before mixing through the white beans and chicken.

Warm through and finish with a drizzle of good oil and a sprinkling of herbs.

Beetroot, Smoked Trout and Toasted Buckwheat

The eastern European flavours in this dish work well with beetroot. You don't need to cook the buckwheat before dry-roasting it. Toasted, it has a completely different taste – it's nutty and crunchy, adding a great texture to the dish. The result is a very pretty pink and brown salad. It's also gluten free.

Serves 4

200g buckwheat
4 teaspoons caraway seeds
5 raw beetroots, peeled and coarsely grated
finely grated zest and juice of 1 orange
6 teaspoons balsamic vinegar
3 tablespoons olive oil
sea salt and freshly ground black pepper
200g smoked trout
1 cucumber, deseeded and sliced
12 radishes, thinly sliced
2 tablespoons dill, chopped

For the dressing:
4 tablespoons crème fraîche
2 tablespoons extra virgin olive oil
juice of 1 lemon
2 tablespoons grated horseradish

Dry-roast the buckwheat in a wide non-stick pan with the caraway seeds until golden brown and fragrant. Allow to cool.

Mix the buckwheat with the grated beetroot, orange zest and juice, balsamic vinegar and olive oil. Season well.

Spread the buckwheat mixture over a large plate. Break up the trout into small pieces and arrange over the top. Scatter the cucumber over.

Make the dressing: mix the crème fraîche with the olive oil, lemon juice and horseradish and season well. Drizzle over the salad.

Finally, sprinkle over the radishes and dill.

Courgette Fritters with Cheese

Ben Bulger works for us in the Field Kitchen. Here are two versions of his original and delicious courgette fritters. They feature heavily as a vegetarian option on the Field Kitchen menu in July. In the second version they are adapted to be gluten-free and vegan, using gram flour – they are still just as tasty.

Serves 6

4 courgettes (about 500g), coarsely grated
sea salt and freshly ground black pepper
6 spring onions, chopped
1 garlic clove, crushed
3 eggs, lightly beaten
250g feta cheese, crumbled
350g fresh soft breadcrumbs
60g Parmesan cheese, grated
100g plain flour
1 chilli, deseeded if preferred, finely chopped
handful of chopped dill and oregano
sunflower oil, for frying

Place the courgettes in a colander over the sink. Salt and leave them for 20 minutes. Squeeze dry.

Put the courgettes in a bowl and add the rest of ingredients, except the sunflower oil. Mix to form a batter. Heat the oil in a large frying pan. Drop in a tablespoon of batter at a time, flattening slightly, and cook for 2–3 minutes on each side until golden brown.

Courgette Fritters

A gluten-free and vegan version.

Serves 6

4 courgettes (about 500g), coarsely grated
sea salt and freshly ground black pepper
120g gram flour
¼ teaspoon bicarbonate of soda
6 spring onions, sliced
2 garlic cloves, finely chopped
1 red chilli, deseeded if preferred, finely chopped
large handfuls of chopped mint and dill
sunflower oil, for frying

Place the courgettes in a colander over the sink. Salt and leave them for 20 minutes. Squeeze dry.

Mix the flour with the bicarbonate of soda, and gradually whisk in about 120ml water to make a batter.

Add the rest of the ingredients, except the sunflower oil.

Shallow-fry in a little oil for 2–3 minutes on each side until golden brown.

Stuffed Courgette Flowers

We generally serve these at the Field Kitchen if we have a special Italian night in the summer. One of our courgette growers likes to bring us flowers, in exchange for a free dinner. You don't have to use the filling just to stuff courgette flowers – it is very good on its own or on toast.

Serves 4

sunflower or mild olive oil, for deep-frying
10–12 courgette flowers, gently brushed clean

For the batter:
2 tablespoons olive oil
150g plain flour
2 egg whites
sea salt and freshly ground black pepper

For the filling:
900g small courgettes
2 tablespoons olive oil
2 heads of garlic, broken into cloves (skins on)
2 tablespoons finely grated Parmesan cheese
juice and zest of 1 unwaxed lemon
2 tablespoons ricotta
1 tablespoon crème fraîche
a little chopped marjoram and parsley

Preheat the oven to 170°C/Gas Mark 4.

Make the batter by whisking the olive oil and flour together and gradually adding lukewarm water until it is the consistency of double cream. Leave to rest for 20 minutes. Stiffly whip the egg whites and fold them into the batter. Season well.

Trim the courgettes and cut them in half lengthways. Toss in the olive oil and place on a baking tray with the garlic cloves, season and roast in the oven for about 40 minutes until cooked and browned. Cool, then squeeze the garlic flesh from the skins. Place the courgettes and garlic in a food processor with all the other ingredients and mix to a smooth paste, then season.

Pour 2–3cm of oil into a deep pan or a deep-fat fryer, and heat until hot (test with a piece of bread, as in the Carrot Fritters recipe on page 166).

Use a dessertspoon to fill the courgette flowers with the filling. Dip them in the batter and deep-fry in batches, making sure not to crowd the pan, until golden brown.

Beetroot Tzatziki

I really like this reinvention of cucumber tzatziki. If you have leftover cooked beetroot it's a good way to use it up; otherwise I would bake the beetroot whole, in their skins, in a fairly hot oven until soft enough to pierce with a knife, then slip the skins off. It's a very summery dish, an amazing bright pink. Delicious just with crispy pitta bread.

Serves 4–6

400g cooked and peeled beetroot
250ml Greek yoghurt
½ red onion, very finely chopped
1 garlic clove, crushed
finely grated zest of 1 orange
1 tablespoon chopped dill
1 tablespoon chopped chives
sea salt and freshly ground black pepper

Grate the beetroot coarsely and mix with the rest of the ingredients. Season well.

Pork Larp

I judge the quality of Thai restaurants by this dish. The toasted ground rice is the defining ingredient, adding a vital crunchy texture. You could use chicken in place of the pork, and the dressing is good with rare beef and sliced duck breast too. The spiciness of the dish is offset by the raw summer vegetables. The ones listed are only a suggestion; use others if you prefer.

Serves 4

2 tablespoons sunflower oil
400g minced pork
1 tablespoon short- or medium-grain rice
½ red onion, finely chopped
1 tablespoon finely sliced lemongrass (use the root end only)
4 tablespoons lime juice
2 tablespoons fish sauce
pinch of cayenne pepper or chilli powder, to taste
leaves from 1 small bunch of mint, roughly chopped
1 tablespoon roughly chopped coriander
1–2 red chillies, deseeded if preferred, finely chopped
sea salt and freshly ground black pepper

For the raw vegetables:
Little Gem or Romaine lettuce, cut into wedges
½ cucumber, sliced
100g sugar snap peas or French beans

Heat the oil in a wok or large frying pan and stir-fry the pork for 5 minutes. Drain on kitchen paper and allow to cool.

Dry-roast the rice in a frying pan, until light brown and smelling toasty. Cool and grind to a powder in a spice grinder or mortar and pestle. Set aside.

Mix the pork mince with the rest of the ingredients (except the toasted ground rice) and check the seasoning.

Mound the pork on a serving plate and surround with the raw vegetables. Sprinkle the pork with the toasted rice. Serve at room temperature.

Sugar Snap Peas and French Beans with Tahini Dressing

You can be flexible about what beans you use in this salad, depending on what's available. You could use French beans on their own, or runner beans instead. Very good with Chermoulah Chicken, Fish or Lamb (see page 254).

Serves 4–6

200g French beans
200g sugar snap peas
2 Little Gem lettuces or other summer salad leaves, washed

For the dressing:
2 tablespoons tahini
2 garlic cloves, crushed
juice of 1 lemon
1 tablespoon chopped coriander or parsley
pinch of paprika
1 tablespoon toasted sesame seeds
sea salt and freshly ground black pepper

Bring two saucepans of water to a boil. Cook the French beans in one pan for 4 minutes until they're squeaky, then refresh in cold water and drain. Blanch the sugar snaps in the other pan for 2 minutes, then refresh and drain.

Mix the dressing ingredients together and add enough water to make it the consistency of single cream. Use it to dress the sugar snaps and beans.

Pull the leaves from the lettuces, place them in a salad bowl and top with the dressed sugar snaps and beans.

Salmon and Soba Noodles

I was lucky enough to work with the chef Peter Gordon in the early days of the Sugar Club restaurant in London. This dish is inspired by my time there. The marinade also works on other oily fish, or steak.

Serves 4

4 salmon fillets, each 100–125g
200g soba noodles
1 teaspoon sesame oil
1 cucumber, peeled, deseeded and sliced
1 bunch of spring onions, chopped
1 tablespoon chopped coriander

For the marinade:
1 tablespoon soy sauce
2 teaspoons oyster sauce
2 teaspoons soft brown sugar
1 tablespoon balsamic vinegar
½ teaspoon five-spice powder
2 teaspoons sesame oil

For the dressing:
2cm piece fresh root ginger, finely chopped or grated
1 garlic clove, crushed
juice of 1–2 limes
2 teaspoons runny honey
75ml sunflower oil
sea salt and freshly ground black pepper

Whisk together the marinade ingredients in a shallow dish and immerse the salmon in it, turning occasionally. Cook the soba noodles in boiling salted water for 10–12 minutes (or according to the packet directions). Drain, refresh in cold water and toss in the sesame oil to prevent them sticking.

Blend together the dressing ingredients in a food processor, or whisk together until thoroughly combined.

Toss the noodles and cucumber in the dressing.

On a hot griddle pan or barbecue, cook the salmon fillets for about 3 minutes on each side depending on their thickness (they taste better if the salmon is slightly pink in the middle).

Place the salmon on the noodles and cucumber and scatter with the spring onions and coriander.

Grilled Lamb and Sugar Snap Salad

Lamb, mint and peas is a classic summery combination. You can use lamb chops instead, but the leg steaks are just as good and a lot cheaper. The salad also works well with cold, leftover roast lamb.

Serves 4

4 lamb leg steaks
1 teaspoon olive oil
300g sugar snap peas
sea salt and freshly ground black pepper
1 bunch of spring onions, chopped
1 bunch of watercress, washed and trimmed

For the dressing:
3 tablespoons rice vinegar
2 teaspoons runny honey
1 tablespoon soy sauce
1 tablespoon sesame oil
1 tablespoon chopped mint

Rub the lamb with a little oil and grill on a hot griddle pan (or barbecue) for 2 minutes on each side. Remove to a warmed plate to rest for 5 minutes.

Meanwhile, blanch the sugar snap peas in boiling salted water for 2 minutes. Drain and refresh in cold water.

Thinly slice the lamb and mix with the sugar snaps, onions and watercress. Whisk together the dressing ingredients and drizzle over the salad.

Vietnamese Spring Rolls and Nuoc Cham Dipping Sauce

This is such a fresh dish and it makes a perfect summer starter or canapé. Cooked chicken or prawns can be added for a more substantial snack and other raw vegetables can be substituted for those here. Constructing the rolls might look a little daunting but it really is quite simple. Make sure the water for the rice paper isn't too hot; it should be just tepid or the paper will break up.

Makes 8

50g vermicelli rice noodles
1 teaspoon sesame oil
8 lettuce leaves (Little Gem or Romaine)
about 24 basil leaves
about 24 mint leaves
8 sprigs of coriander
1 carrot, cut into fine strips
½ red pepper, cut into fine strips
¼ cucumber, deseeded and cut into fine strips
6 sugar snap peas, cut into fine strips
6 radishes, cut into fine strips
8 rice paper wrappers

For the nuoc cham dipping sauce:
1 teaspoon rice vinegar
1 tablespoon caster sugar
2 red chillies, deseeded if preferred, chopped
2 garlic cloves, chopped
2 tablespoons fish sauce (or light soy sauce for veggies)
juice of 1 lime

First make the dipping sauce. In a saucepan, bring the vinegar, sugar and 3 tablespoons water to a boil. Cool, then add the rest of the ingredients.

Cook the noodles for 3–4 minutes, or until al dente. Drain and refresh. Cut them into smaller pieces and toss in the sesame oil. Lay out each lettuce leaf, top with 3 leaves each of basil and mint, a sprig of coriander, the strips of vegetables and the noodles.

Soak one rice paper wrapper in warm water until soft and pliable. Place on a damp cloth and top with the filled lettuce leaf, then roll up as tightly as possible, folding in the sides to make a parcel. Repeat with the other rice papers and lettuce leaves.

To serve, slice the rolls in half diagonally and serve with the dipping sauce.

Bean and Fennel Salad

This is a lovely salad in which to use early fennel. It is great served with Confit of Salmon (see page 150) or any grilled fish. Try adding slow-roasted tomatoes, black olives or shredded basil as well.

Serves 4

200g French beans, trimmed
200g runner beans, trimmed and chopped
1 head of fennel, very finely shaved on a mandolin
1 garlic clove, crushed
3 tablespoons good-quality extra virgin olive oil
1 tablespoon lemon juice
sea salt and freshly ground black pepper

Bring a pan of water to a boil. Blanch the French and runner beans for 2–3 minutes, then refresh in cold water and drain.

While still hot, toss the beans in a bowl with the fennel, garlic, oil and lemon juice. Season well.

John Dory as in Sicily

This is a recipe from Mitch Tonks, the expert we know as 'Mr Fish'. He owns two fantastic restaurants, the Seahorse and Rockfish Seafood and Chips, in Dartmouth. This recipe can also be tried with gurnard, Dover sole or megrim.

Serves 2–3

1 John Dory, about 750g
100ml good-quality olive oil
50ml white wine
10 small black olives
3 ripe tomatoes, skinned
1 tablespoon capers
small handful of chopped parsley
small handful of fine breadcrumbs
squeeze of lemon juice
sea salt

Preheat the oven to 250°C/Gas Mark 9.

Place the fish in a roasting dish and drizzle over the olive oil and wine. Add the olives and squeeze the tomatoes over the fish so you release the juices and break up the flesh, then add the capers. Sprinkle half the chopped parsley and all the breadcrumbs over the fish, then roast in the oven for 20 minutes. During the wild garlic season add a few leaves of wild garlic under and over the fish.

Remove from the oven and finish off with a good squeeze of lemon, some salt and a final sprinkling of parsley.

Blackcurrant Mess

This is a quick summer dessert. I really like the sharpness of blackcurrants, and it's nice to have the mixture of cooked and uncooked textures. You could add some fresh custard to make it a little more like a fool. Instead of ready-made meringues, it's rewarding to make your own – you could use the Brown Sugar Meringues recipe on page 314.

Serves 4

300g blackcurrants
3 tablespoons caster sugar
1 tablespoon crème de cassis or brandy
400ml whipping cream
4 ready-made meringue nests
200ml cold custard (optional)

Mix half the blackcurrants with half the sugar and all the cassis or brandy and leave to macerate.

Cook the other half of the blackcurrants with the remaining sugar and 100ml water until syrupy. Cool.

Whip the cream until soft peaks form. In a large bowl, break the meringue nests and fold through the cream. Drizzle the custard over (if using).

Combine the two blackcurrant mixes together and pour over the meringues and cream. Fold together roughly, leaving a ripple effect. Transfer to a serving bowl.

SUNDAY

Lamb Cooked in Milk with Fennel

This is an elegant, fragrant dish. Based on a recipe by Marlene Blasi, it's a southern Italian classic. Traditionally, young lamb would have been cooked in ewe's milk. Lamb shoulder or leg works well, but the dish needs a bit of fat, so it's important to add some cream. Reduce the cooking juices at the end for an accompanying sauce.

Serves 6

3 tablespoons fennel seeds, ground
3 tablespoons chopped parsley
3 garlic cloves, crushed
3 tablespoons olive oil
1kg lamb shoulder or leg, trimmed and cut into 5–6cm chunks
sea salt and freshly ground black pepper
700ml milk
200ml double cream
1 tablespoon chopped fennel tops, wild fennel or dill

Mix together the fennel seeds, parsley and garlic.

Heat the olive oil in a large pan until hot, and brown half the lamb. Remove the lamb from the pan, reduce the heat and add the fennel seed mixture. Cook gently without colouring. Add the remaining lamb and brown it in the fennel paste. Return the rest of the lamb to the pan with its juices and add 1 teaspoon of salt.

Add a little of the milk, using it to scrape any residue from around the pan. Add the rest of the milk and the cream and bring to a very gentle simmer. Cover with a round of baking parchment and leave just simmering for 1–1½ hours, until the meat is tender.

Remove the meat from the pan, cover and set aside. Reduce the pan juices on a high heat until slightly thickened.

Return the lamb to the pan, season and sprinkle with the herbs.

Hispi Cabbage, Summer Greens, Broad Beans and Lentils

This is a very fresh-looking dish using the best greens available at this time of year, combined with broad beans and a few lentils. Summer greens have quite a short season, but chard can be used instead. You can add spring onions right at the end of cooking, if you like.

Serves 4–6

150g broad beans, shelled weight
25g unsalted butter
2 tablespoons olive oil
1 Hispi cabbage, cored and finely shredded
1 bunch of summer greens, shredded
2 tablespoons cooked Puy lentils
1 garlic clove, crushed
sea salt and freshly ground black pepper
extra virgin olive oil, to serve
handful of shredded mint or basil

Blanch the broad beans in a large pan of boiling water for 3 minutes or until tender. Drain.

Melt the butter and half the olive oil in a large pan. When hot, add the Hispi and cook quickly, stirring all the time, for 2 minutes. Add the summer greens and continue to cook for 5 minutes, until wilted. Add the broad beans, lentils and garlic. Mix well and season.

Cook for a few more minutes until the cabbage is tender. Remove from the heat, drizzle with extra virgin olive oil and scatter with herbs.

Artichoke Gratin

This is another southern Italian dish, and it's very good with the Lamb Cooked in Milk (page 183). It's tricky in the Field Kitchen to cook a pure artichoke dish when we have a full house, as they're so labour-intensive. However, I have been known to take a crate of artichokes home to prepare in front of the TV. If you keep them in acidulated (lemony) water, you can prepare the night before.

Serves 4–6

4 globe artichokes
finely grated zest and juice of 2 unwaxed lemons
2 garlic cloves, crushed
3 tablespoons breadcrumbs
2 tablespoons grated Parmesan or pecorino cheese
1 tablespoon chopped marjoram
1 tablespoon chopped parsley
sea salt and freshly ground black pepper
2 tablespoons white wine
2 tablespoons olive oil

Preheat the oven to 180°C/Gas Mark 4.

Trim the artichokes: peel off the coarse petals. Cut the woody ends from the stems and peel the tender lengths, then trim around the bases. Remove the furry 'chokes' in the middle of the artichokes and cut each into 8 wedges. Place the trimmed artichokes in a bowl of water acidulated with a little of the lemon juice, to stop discoloration.

Mix the garlic, breadcrumbs, cheese, herbs and lemon zest together and season well.

Mix the remaining lemon juice and white wine together.

Drain the artichokes and place in an ovenproof gratin dish. Season and sprinkle with the breadcrumb topping mix. Pour the white wine and lemon juice down the side of the dish and drizzle the oil over the top. Bake in the oven for 30–40 minutes, until the top is browned and the artichokes are tender.

Apricot Brioche Pudding

Based on a Chez Panisse recipe, this is a great take on a classic bread and butter pudding. It can be made with fresh apricots only in the summer – we import ours from France whose Orange Red and Bergeron varieties are particularly good – but in the winter you can use dried. For the best flavour, combine the two. The caramelised base is the best bit.

Serves 8–10

125g dried apricots
450g caster sugar
250g fresh apricots, halved and pitted
7 egg yolks
500ml milk
250ml double cream
250g tub crème fraîche
finely grated zest of 1 orange
few drops of vanilla extract
few drops of almond extract
grated nutmeg
1 tablespoon ground almonds
2 tablespoons apricot brandy
500g brioche, cut into 2cm chunks

Preheat the oven to 160°C/Gas Mark 3.

Cut the dried apricots into very thin slices and simmer in 250ml water and 100g of the sugar for 10 minutes. Add the fresh apricots and simmer for 5 more minutes. Drain the fruit, then return the cooking liquor to the pan with 250g more sugar and 125ml more water. Boil the liquid until it caramelises slightly to a light brown colour, then pour into a 2-litre shallow pudding dish.

Whisk the egg yolks and add the rest of the ingredients except the remaining sugar and the brioche. Mix well. Gently stir in the apricots and brioche pieces. Transfer to the pudding dish. Sprinkle with the remaining sugar. Place the pudding dish in a deep roasting tray and pour in enough water to come halfway up the sides of the dish. Cook in the oven for about 45 minutes until golden and lightly set.

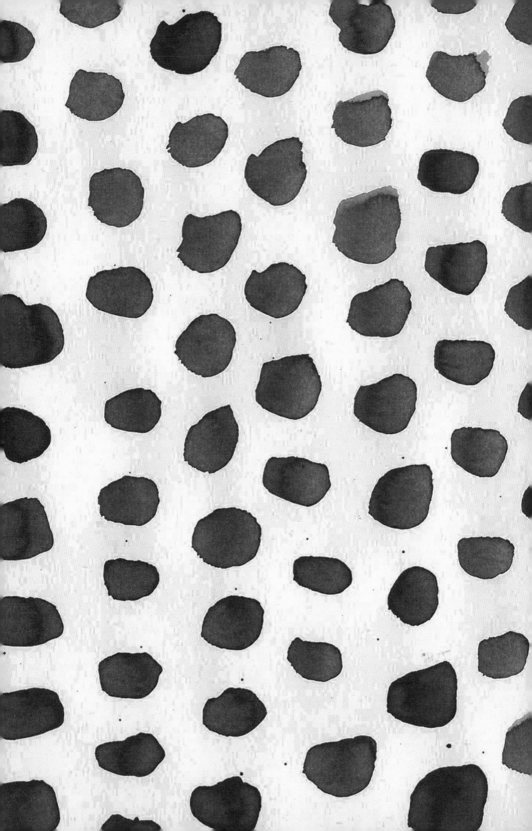

Everyday

Spaghetti with Zucchini
Risotto Cake
French Beans in Red Pepper Dressing
French and Runner Beans with Sun-dried
Tomatoes, Olives and Basil
Salmon with Cherry Tomatoes and Olives
Cheesy Beans
Fish Wrapped in Lettuce
Pasta with Tomatoes and Rocket
Basic Tomato Sauce
Spaghetti with Fresh Tomatoes and Almond Pesto
Tomato and Ginger Sauce with Cardamom
Rocket Salad with Coppa di Parma, Semi-dried Tomatoes and Pecorino
Acqua e Sale ('Water and Salt')
Parsley Salad
Cachumber Salad
Pasta with Runner Beans and Smoked Salmon
Italian Farro Salad with Vegetables and Pesto

Sunday

Lamb Involtini
French Beans with Anchovy and Tomato
Roast Carrot Salad with Lentils and Goat's Cheese
Franco's Italian Summer Pudding

AUGUST

Easy pickings

August sees the vegetable season at its peak, and our veg boxes full of flavour and variety as summer meets early autumn and growing is easy. With light levels still good, the tunnels are bursting, with tomatoes, peppers, aubergine, cucumbers, chillies and basil all at their best. Outside we see an abundance of summer salads and roots and the arrival of early crops of sweetcorn, broccoli and a few leeks. The English apple season starts with the wonderfully perfumed Discovery; you need to catch it just right, as this variety goes from excessively tart through perfection to woolly in just a few days.

Tomatoes: reliably bland or unpredictably wonderful

From our farm in France we have wonderfully sweet Charentais melons and, if all goes well, outdoor-grown tomatoes and peppers – a little unpredictable in appearance but with a flavour that leaves crops grown under plastic and glass (99 per cent of the commercial crop) in the shade. When we asked our professional tomato-growing neighbours in the Vendée how to produce a really good tomato, each of them took us out of their greenhouses, full of perfectly shaped fruit, and round the back to the rows of irregular plants exposed to whatever nature threw at them. There was a broad acceptance amongst these professionals that if you wanted flavour you had to grow outside and accept the less reliable results. As is so often the case, the quest for yield, consistency and cosmetic perfection that inevitably results from supplying supermarkets was incompatible with culinary virtue. I have seen the same in the UK, where commercial growers do not eat what they sell to supermarkets, but have a vegetable plot for themselves around the back, which is organic in all but name. It remains to be seen whether growing tomatoes and peppers outside can make commercial sense for Riverford but we are having a go.

Eating the courgette mountain

Courgettes produce their first fruits in late June, by the end of July they are cropping so heavily that we struggle to keep up with them, and by August, much as we loved them a month ago, with so much other veg around we dread their arrival at the barn doors. Jane deep-fries the flowers (see page 172), perhaps still attached to small fruits (up to 70mm). These are hard to find in the shops because they have such a short shelf life, making this a gardener's treat. The smaller male flowers can also be used without reducing yield, though after a month with even three or four plants you may feel your kitchen is a slave to cucurbit fecundity and be happy to curtail their

production for a few days. Before stuffing, check carefully for slugs, which seem to like to sleep in there. My favourite way of eating the courgette mountain is as courgette fritters topped with a freshly made salsa – cheap and dead easy to make and I have yet to find anyone who didn't love them. Try Jane's variations on pages 170 and 171, and try your own versions with fresh chillies and herbs too.

Do not be tempted to stockpile courgettes; when truly fresh, they have a wonderful flavour, but their reputation suffers from their deceptive ability to look fresh even when they have been kept in the high-humidity cold room for weeks. This is what tends to happen as the glut comes on: growers and wholesalers 'manage' or rotate their stock, hoping for an upturn in sales that seldom comes. They may look OK but they have lost all trace of flavour and most of their nutritional value. Use courgettes fresh or chuck them on the compost heap.

Gluts and allotments

Sadly for Riverford, August is also the month when the nation deserts the kitchen and our sales take a dive. Some are away on holiday, some are at home on holiday but don't want to cook and, increasingly in recent years, some are in the allotment or garden growing their own. Philosophically, I wholeheartedly support this movement to get connected with, and take back control of, our food; business-wise, though, with over half of our customers now growing some of their own, it poses us some difficulties and we have to plan carefully to avoid gluts. On the bright side, having got their hands in the soil and tasted the real thing, with all the wonderful irregularity and tolerable blemishes that nature produces (before a pack house grades it out), gardening customers find it hard to go back to the bland and shiny uniformity of over-packaged anonymous supermarket veg and generally return to Riverford in the autumn. On the bad side, they tend, as our climate dictates, to be growing the same crops as us and to be sharing the bounty with their box-buying neighbours. To rub salt in the wound, we get a rash of midsummer emails from customers citing bumper crops of runner beans as their reason for cancelling boxes. I get the distinct impression that I am expected to congratulate them while ours hang abandoned in the field. Sour grapes? Definitely. Rather than sulking over our unwanted beans, with planting coming to an end and time on our hands, we throw a big party by the irrigation lake and try to eat as much as we can ourselves.

One could be eating Brussels sprouts, swedes, parsnips and kale, though I can never understand why anyone would want to eat winter foods in August when summer will be gone soon enough. French beans are at their peak and I could eat them every day. Thankfully, the craze for baby veg seems to have largely passed. If you want those tiny, matchstick-thin bobby beans, you can grow them yourself or they are going to be air-freighted from a low-wage economy, even in August; no one can afford to pick them in this country and they really don't taste any better. We go for the longest, fattest, most flavoursome varieties we can find to keep picking costs down.

Quick and easy ideas
TOMATOES

Quick and easy ideas
TOMATOES

Insalata caprese

Slice good-quality mozzarella and serve with sliced ripe tomatoes. Sprinkle with torn basil, salt and olive oil.

Tomato and courgette gratin

Toss slices of courgette with a little pesto to coat. Layer alternately with tomato in an ovenproof dish, seasoning as you go. Top with a few breadcrumbs and some cheese. Drizzle with olive oil and bake in a medium oven for 30 minutes until the veg is tender.

Stuffed tomatoes

Cut in half and scoop out the pulp and seeds. Mix a little ricotta with chopped herbs and some beaten egg. Season well and add a little grated nutmeg. Finely chopped salami can also be added. Stuff the tomatoes with the mixture. Sprinkle with breadcrumbs and bake in a medium oven for 30 minutes.

Bruschetta

Combine chopped tomatoes, chopped anchovies, capers, crushed garlic and torn basil. Grill some sourdough slices, rub with garlic and drizzle with olive oil. Season the tomato mixture and use to top the bread, then drizzle with more good olive oil to serve.

Slow-roasted tomatoes

Cut cherry tomatoes in half. Place on a baking tray cut-side up. Drizzle with olive oil and season with salt and pepper. Cook slowly in a low oven (120°C/ Gas Mark 1) for 1½–2 hours.

Spaghetti with Zucchini

There is a lovely village around the coast from Sorrento where I have twice camped with my son. This is the very local pasta dish; a version appears on every restaurant menu.

Serves 4

1kg courgettes (zucchini)
3 tablespoons olive oil, plus more to serve
100g Parmesan cheese, finely grated
100g pecorino cheese, finely grated
good handful of basil leaves, shredded
50g unsalted butter, softened
sea salt and freshly ground black pepper
350g spaghetti, spaghettini, linguine or penne

Cut the courgettes in half lengthways and slice thinly. Fry in batches with the olive oil, a few at a time, until they are golden in colour. Put in a large pan with the cheeses, basil, butter – cut into knobs – and seasoning.

Cook the pasta according to the packet directions until al dente. Reserve a little of the cooking liquor. Drain the pasta and mix with the courgettes and cheese, adding the reserved pasta water to help combine everything. Season, drizzle with olive oil and serve.

Risotto Cake

I had to make this to feed four hundred, when I worked for a production company in London. But it makes a great vegetarian main course for a much smaller number of people. Use any summery vegetables you like in the filling – we've tried grilled fennel, spinach and even the first leeks of the year. You don't have to eat it immediately; it tastes just as good at room temperature for a picnic.

Serves 6

1 onion, finely chopped
2 tablespoons olive oil, plus more for the vegetables
pinch of saffron
½ teaspoon ground fennel seeds
2 garlic cloves, crushed
pinch of chilli flakes
2 tablespoons drained tinned chopped tomatoes, or fresh peeled chopped
    tomatoes
300g risotto rice
sea salt and freshly ground black pepper
splash of white wine or vermouth
1 litre hot vegetable or chicken stock
leaves from 1 bunch of basil, finely shredded
1 aubergine, thinly sliced
2 courgettes, thinly sliced
butter, for the tin
125g mozzarella cheese, sliced
100g peeled red peppers, or piquillo peppers
1 tablespoon grated Parmesan cheese

In a large saucepan or sauté pan, cook the onion in the olive oil with the saffron for 10 minutes over a low heat. Add the fennel seeds, garlic and chilli and cook for another couple of minutes before adding the chopped tomatoes and rice. Increase the heat and cook for 5 minutes, simmering vigorously. Season well and add the wine. In a separate pan, bring the stock to a simmer.

Stir the rice well and start to add the hot stock a ladle at a time over a medium heat, adding more only when the last addition has been absorbed, but before the rice starts to stick. When the majority of the liquid has been used, check

the texture of the rice (it should be almost cooked but still have a little bite to it). Check the seasoning, add the basil, stir and allow to cool.

Preheat the oven to 180°C/Gas Mark 4.

Toss the aubergine and courgette slices in a little olive oil, season and grill on a hot griddle pan or barbecue until there are char lines visible and the vegetables are soft to the touch. Butter a terrine or loaf tin and line the base with a strip of baking parchment.

Press one-third of the cooled rice into the bottom of the mould, then layer on half the courgettes, aubergine, mozzarella and red peppers. Sprinkle with the Parmesan. Repeat, then finish with a final layer of rice.

Place in the oven for about 30 minutes, until golden brown on top. Remove and run around the edge with a knife before turning out on to a warmed serving dish.

Serve sliced, either hot or cold.

French Beans in Red Pepper Dressing

This red pepper dressing makes a fabulous dip for bread or crudités. You could also use it to dress a whole variety of vegetables: runner beans, cauliflower, romanesco or corn.

Serves 4–6

200g French beans, topped and tailed
sea salt

For the dressing:
4 red peppers, deseeded and roughly chopped
3 red onions, roughly chopped
4 garlic cloves
4 large tomatoes
1 teaspoon fennel seeds
1 teaspoon coriander seeds
1 teaspoon cumin seeds
pinch of chilli flakes
2 tablespoons caster sugar
3 tablespoons balsamic vinegar
slug of olive oil
handful of fresh coriander leaves

Preheat the oven to 200°C/Gas Mark 6.

For the dressing, roast all the ingredients except the coriander leaves together for 30 minutes, until caramelised in texture. Blitz the roasted mixture in a food processor.

Blanch the beans for 5 minutes in boiling salted water, then drain.

Toss the beans in the dressing, sprinkle with the coriander and serve.

French and Runner Beans with Sun-dried Tomatoes, Olives and Basil

French and runner beans tend to work well when dressed with something slightly salty – as with the olives in this recipe. Later in the season, you could use runner beans on their own or add some early leeks. Also try this tomato and olive mixture added to tomato pasta sauce.

Serves 6

200g French beans, topped and tailed
100g runner beans, thinly sliced
sea salt and freshly ground black pepper
5 sun-dried tomatoes, finely chopped
1 tablespoon black olives, pitted and chopped
handful of basil leaves, shredded
1 tablespoon extra virgin olive oil

Blanch both types of beans in boiling salted water for about 5 minutes until cooked (not al dente but squeaky when bitten).

Meanwhile, mix together all the rest of the ingredients in a bowl.

Drain the beans well and toss while still hot in the bowl with the olive mixture. Check the seasoning and serve.

Salmon with Cherry Tomatoes and Olives

Franco Taruschio (who used to own the Walnut Tree in Abergavenny) and Christine Smallwood hosted a night of food and stories at the Field Kitchen – this was the main course. It is very easy and quick to make, and good served on a bed of cannellini beans, French beans, thinly sliced red onions and raw shaved fennel tossed in olive oil with chopped parsley and a touch of garlic lightly fried in olive oil. At the Field Kitchen we use sustainable Loch Duart salmon.

Serves 4

2 tablespoons extra virgin olive oil
4 skinless salmon fillets, each about 125g
20 small cherry tomatoes on the vine
16–20 black olives (preferably Gaeta)
sea salt and freshly ground black pepper
2 tablespoons balsamic vinegar

Preheat the oven to 200°C/Gas Mark 6.

Heat the oil in an ovenproof frying pan and fry the salmon pieces briefly on both sides. Add the tomatoes and olives and season. Cover and put in the oven for a few minutes to finish cooking.

Drizzle balsamic vinegar on top of the salmon.

Cheesy Beans

This is a really quick and tasty recipe for French or runner beans. Serve with something fresh and sweet – such as a tomato and basil salad.

Serves 4

300g French beans or runner beans (or a mixture)
sea salt and freshly ground black pepper
50g unsalted butter
2 tablespoons finely grated Parmesan cheese
2 tablespoons grated melting cheese, such as Fontina or Gruyère

Cook the beans in boiling salted water for 5 minutes or until just cooked, then drain. In a large pan, melt the butter gently.

Add the beans to the butter and season. Toss well, add the cheeses and mix. Cover and remove from the heat for a few minutes before serving.

Fish Wrapped in Lettuce

Once the paste is made, this dish is simple to put together. Wet the lettuce leaves just before using so they haven't dried out before you start wrapping the fish. Cooked fresh green vegetables, such as French beans or calabrese, can be added to the broth. The fish can be cooked the same way but without the paste, substituting fresh summer herbs and finishing the sauce with a little cream. Serve with basmati rice.

Serves 4

1 Cos or Romaine lettuce
4 x 175g pieces firm white fish (gurnard, brill or farmed sea bream)
1 red onion, finely chopped
300ml hot fish stock
2 teaspoons fish sauce

For the paste:
2cm piece fresh root ginger, grated
zest of 1 unwaxed lemon
2 garlic cloves, crushed
1 red chilli, deseeded if preferred, finely chopped
1 teaspoon turmeric
1 tablespoon chopped coriander stalks
1 bunch of spring onions, finely chopped
75g creamed coconut, grated

Preheat the oven to 180°C/Gas Mark 4.

Remove 8 leaves from the lettuce and pour boiling water over them in a colander in the sink. Refresh immediately in cold water, cut out and discard the thick central rib from each and lay the leaves out on a clean cloth.

Make a paste by mixing all the paste ingredients together and blitzing briefly in a food processor until well combined.

Spread out 2 lettuce leaves, place a piece of fish on them and spread the spice paste over. Repeat to use all the lettuce and fish, reserving 1 teaspoon of the paste.

Roll up the lettuce parcels, folding in the sides to seal. Place the fish parcels on top of the onion in an ovenproof dish. Pour in the hot stock and fish sauce and place in the oven for 15 minutes.

When cooked, place the fish parcels on a warmed serving dish. Transfer their juices to a pan and whisk in the reserved paste. Serve poured around the fish, with greens and rice.

Pasta with Tomatoes and Rocket

This pasta sauce is typical of Puglia and quick and easy to make. You can use any very ripe, very sweet tomatoes. Traditionally, cacioricotta, a type of hard ricotta, is used in Puglia, but you can substitute any type of hard ricotta (such as ricotta salata), pecorino or, failing those, feta.

Serves 4

1kg cherry tomatoes
3 tablespoons olive oil
3 garlic cloves, crushed
sea salt and freshly ground black pepper
350g farfalle, fusilli or orecchiette
2 bunches of rocket (about 200g), washed and roughly chopped
100g hard ricotta cheese, coarsely grated or shaved

Cut the cherry tomatoes into quarters and cook in the oil with the garlic and seasoning for 5 minutes.

Cook the pasta for about 10 minutes in boiling salted water (or according to the packet directions) until almost cooked. Drain and return to the pan with the fresh tomato sauce. Mix well and add the rocket leaves; they will wilt through the sauce.

Season well and serve topped with the cheese.

Basic Tomato Sauce

An easy tomato sauce for when you have a glut. (In the winter, you can make the same recipe with tinned tomatoes.) It can be adapted to include other ingredients such as basil, chilli, rosemary or pancetta.

Serves 4

450g good, ripe tomatoes
2 tablespoons olive oil
4 garlic cloves, finely chopped
1 teaspoon caster sugar
sea salt and freshly ground black pepper

Peel the tomatoes by making a small slash on each, putting them in a dish and pouring boiling water over them. Leave for 30 seconds, then refresh with cold water. The skins should come away easily. Remove the hard cores, squeeze out and discard the seeds and chop up the flesh.

Heat the olive oil in a heavy-based pan, add the garlic and cook gently for a few minutes until softened but not coloured.

Stir in the tomatoes and sugar and increase the heat until the tomatoes are simmering.

Reduce the heat once more and cook gently for about 1 hour, until reduced and thickening.

Season well.

Spaghetti with Fresh Tomatoes and Almond Pesto

A variation on a classic pesto, this is based on a Sicilian pasta dish. Use the best and ripest tomatoes you can.

Serves 4

500g ripe tomatoes
sea salt and freshly ground black pepper
2 garlic cloves, crushed
leaves from 1 small bunch of basil
30g flaked (or whole blanched) almonds, lightly toasted
3 tablespoons good-quality olive oil, plus a little more
75g pecorino cheese, finely grated
350g spaghetti

Peel the tomatoes by making a small slash on each, putting them in a dish and pouring boiling water over them. Leave for 30 seconds, then refresh with cold water. The skins should come away easily. Remove the hard cores, squeeze out the seeds and chop up the flesh. Set the chopped tomatoes aside, sprinkled with a little salt.

In a food processor, grind together the garlic, basil and almonds with the olive oil. If you can't adapt your food processor to a smaller capacity, try using a stick blender with a bowl attachment, or grind by hand in a pestle and mortar. Transfer to a bowl, stir and add the pecorino, chopped tomatoes and more olive oil. Season.

Cook the spaghetti in boiling salted water until al dente. Drain and toss through the tomato mixture. Season.

Tomato and Ginger Sauce with Cardamom

This fragrant sauce is perfect with simply cooked fish and braised spinach.

Makes 200ml/Serves 4–6

1 onion, finely chopped
4–6cm piece fresh root ginger, finely grated
5 garlic cloves, crushed
1 teaspoon sea salt
3 tablespoons sunflower oil
pinch of turmeric
pinch of cayenne pepper
1 clove, ground
seeds from 4 cardamom pods, ground
10 ripe tomatoes, skinned and chopped (see page 207)
1 tablespoon chopped coriander

Cook the onion, ginger, garlic and salt slowly in the oil for 20 minutes, softening but not colouring the ingredients.

Add the spices and tomatoes and cook for another 15 minutes.

Check the seasoning and stir in the chopped coriander.

Rocket Salad with Coppa di Parma, Semi-dried Tomatoes and Pecorino

This is a 'chuck it all together' salad – there's no need to be too exact about the quantities and the ingredients are flexible too. If you don't have any coppa, use Serrano or Parma ham; you could also use flaked almonds in place of the pine nuts.

Serves 4

150g rocket, trimmed and washed
2 heads bitter leaves such as chicory, endive or radicchio, separated
¼ red onion, thinly sliced
10 slices coppa di Parma, or Parma or Serrano ham, cut into thin strips
10 semi-dried tomatoes, thinly sliced
10 basil leaves, roughly torn
1 tablespoon pine nuts, toasted
50g pecorino cheese, shaved

For the dressing:
3 tablespoons extra virgin olive oil
1 tablespoon red wine vinegar
pinch of nutmeg
sea salt and freshly ground black pepper

In a salad bowl, place the rocket, bitter leaves, onion, coppa di Parma, tomatoes, basil, and half the pine nuts and pecorino.

Mix together the oil, vinegar, nutmeg, salt and pepper. Toss together with the salad ingredients.

Scatter with the remaining pine nuts and pecorino.

Acqua e Sale ('Water and Salt')

This comes from the restaurant Antichi Sapori in Andria; the recipe is adapted from *An Appetite for Puglia* by Christine Smallwood, a regular visitor to the Field Kitchen. It is typical of the many ways that stale bread is used up with seasonal vegetables in Italy. Don't prepare it too far in advance – the bread should retain some of its crunch.

Serves 4

10 cherry tomatoes, halved
½ garlic clove, finely chopped
1 small red onion, thinly sliced
½ cucumber, peeled, halved lengthways and thinly sliced
sea salt and freshly ground black pepper
large handful of chopped parsley
leaves from a few sprigs of oregano, chopped
extra virgin olive oil
300g old dry bread, cut into small cubes

In a large bowl, put the tomatoes, garlic, onion, cucumber, salt, pepper, parsley, oregano and enough oil to coat everything generously, and mix well.

Separately, sprinkle half a glass of water over the bread, then mix the bread with the vegetables, so that it is covered in oil.

As soon as the bread starts to soften, serve.

Parsley Salad

This salad is good served on crostini, mixed with cooked orzo pasta, or as a side dish with grilled chicken or fish.

Serves 4–6

50g flat-leaf parsley, chopped
50g red onion, finely chopped
2 tablespoons capers, rinsed
12 anchovy fillets, finely chopped
50g sun-dried tomatoes, finely chopped
finely grated zest and juice of 1 unwaxed lemon
4 tablespoons extra virgin olive oil
sea salt and freshly ground black pepper

Mix all the ingredients together well and season.

Cachumber Salad

This is a great salad to serve with spicy fish dishes, Indian food or simply on toast for a healthy snack.

Serves 4–6

200g tomatoes, chopped
1 onion, finely chopped
4 tablespoons chopped coriander, parsley or mint
½ teaspoon cumin seeds, roasted and ground
½ teaspoon cayenne pepper
2 tablespoons balsamic vinegar
¾ teaspoon salt

Combine all the ingredients together in a bowl.

Pasta with Runner Beans and Smoked Salmon

The smoked salmon sauce is very moreish, and can be made with the trimmings so that it's not too expensive. It is quite rich, but the runner beans freshen and lighten it. The sauce can also be used as a dressing for cooked mussels – reduce the mussel cooking liquor and add to the sauce before serving.

Serves 4

200g runner beans, topped and tailed
1 tablespoon olive oil
1 red pepper, deseeded and finely chopped
2 teaspoons chopped rosemary
1 garlic clove, crushed
200ml double cream
100g smoked salmon trimmings, thinly sliced
200g tagliolini or tagliatelle
sea salt and freshly ground black pepper
1 tablespoon finely grated Parmesan cheese

Cut the runner beans into thin strips lengthways and set aside.

Pour the olive oil into a sauté pan, place over a medium heat and cook the red pepper slowly for 10 minutes. Add the rosemary and garlic and cook for 1 minute before adding the cream. Bring to a boil. Remove from the heat and add the smoked salmon.

Drop the pasta into boiling salted water and cook for about 8 minutes (or according to the packet directions). When there are just 3 minutes to go, drop the runner beans into the water and cook until the pasta is al dente. Drain the runner beans and pasta and toss with the sauce.

Season and sprinkle with Parmesan.

Italian Farro Salad with Vegetables and Pesto

Farro wheat is traditionally used in salads in Tuscany. It has an interesting texture and can be combined with a variety of summer vegetables and dressings. This one uses pesto, but a basic olive oil and vinegar dressing can be substituted. Use a home-made pesto or buy a good one like Riverford's, made by Giancarlo Ceci, who also grows calabrese for us. If you can't get hold of farro, short- or medium-grain brown rice will also work.

Serves 4

100g farro, soaked overnight in cold water
sea salt and freshly ground black pepper
1 tablespoon extra virgin olive oil
150g potatoes, cut into 1cm cubes
100g green beans, sliced into 1cm pieces
100g courgettes, cut into small pieces
10 cherry tomatoes, quartered
2 teaspoons pesto

Cook the farro in 500ml boiling water for 10 minutes (if you haven't pre-soaked the farro, it will take 30–40 minutes). Drain, season, toss in the olive oil and leave to cool.

Cook the potatoes in boiling water for 10 minutes and the green beans and courgettes for 4 minutes. Drain, season and allow to cool. Mix with the farro, tomatoes and pesto.

Check the seasoning and serve.

SUNDAY

Lamb Involtini

This is based on a dish cooked at the Agriturismo Il Frantoio near Otranto in Puglia. On our first visit to the area, we stayed there and sampled one of their tasting dinners, shared by the table just as at the Field Kitchen. It was cooked by Rosalba, and it was an amazing experience. The original dish was slow-cooked lamb, for Easter, but the flavours transfer well to the speedier rolled lamb leg steaks.

Serves 6

6 lamb leg steaks
juice of 2 lemons
3 tablespoons olive oil
1 teaspoon freshly ground black pepper
200ml chicken stock

For the paste:
2 garlic cloves, crushed
2 tablespoons drained tinned chopped tomatoes
1½ tablespoons finely grated Parmesan cheese
2 tablespoons finely chopped parsley
sea salt and freshly ground black pepper

Pound the lamb leg steaks between pieces of greaseproof paper until flattened to double the area. Marinate them at room temperature in the lemon juice, 2 tablespoons of the olive oil and the black pepper for at least 1 hour.

Whiz the ingredients for the paste in a food processor and season.

Lay out the marinated leg steaks. Spread the paste over each piece of lamb and roll up tightly. Secure with cocktail sticks.

Heat the remaining olive oil in a non-stick frying pan until very hot, and brown the lamb all over for about 5 minutes, turning occasionally to ensure even cooking. Season.

Remove from the pan and leave on a plate to rest for 10 minutes. Pour the stock into the pan and reduce until slightly thickened.

The lamb can be served as is or sliced with the sauce poured over.

French Beans with Anchovy and Tomato

On a recent visit to Puglia we ate at the Da Bufi restaurant in Molfetta, and lunch kicked off with an inspirational selection of vegetable-based antipasti. One that particularly stood out was French beans with salt cod and tomato. Here we've replaced the salt cod with an anchovy dressing, but you could still add it in if you like. French beans can be replaced with runner beans. This would be a good accompaniment to grilled fish.

Serves 4

300g French beans, trimmed
2 tablespoons olive oil
1 garlic clove, crushed
1 red chilli, deseeded if preferred, finely chopped
6 anchovy fillets
10 cherry tomatoes, quartered
sea salt and freshly ground black pepper
drizzle of extra virgin olive oil

Blanch the French beans in boiling salted water for about 6 minutes, until just cooked or squeaky when bitten through. Meanwhile, heat the oil in a large pan.

Add the garlic, chilli and anchovy to the olive oil. When sizzling, remove from the heat and beat vigorously until the anchovies 'melt' into the other ingredients.

Drain the beans well and transfer to the anchovy dressing; toss until the beans are well coated with the seasoned oil.

Add the tomatoes, season well and serve drizzled with a little extra virgin olive oil.

Roast Carrot Salad with Lentils and Goat's Cheese

New season carrots taste very good when roasted, and don't need to be cooked for too long. This salad will be just as successful with some new beetroot, roasted in its skin then peeled, added to or instead of the carrots. To cook the Puy lentils, put them in a large pan with enough water to cover by 2cm, add some peeled cloves of garlic, bring to a boil and simmer until tender (about 20 minutes). Drain the lentils, and dress with some oil and seasoning while still warm.

Serves 4–6

½ red onion, finely chopped
1 tablespoon red wine vinegar
2 teaspoons brown sugar
1 bunch of new carrots, washed, trimmed and halved lengthways
2 tablespoons olive oil
1 teaspoon honey
sea salt and freshly ground black pepper
3 tablespoons cooked Puy lentils
1 garlic clove, crushed
2 pitta breads, or other flatbreads
100g salad leaves, or 1 bunch of watercress
100g hard goat's cheese, or 3 tablespoons goat's cheese dressing (see
    page 114)

Preheat the oven to 180°C/Gas Mark 4.

First of all, soak the red onion in the vinegar and sugar. Toss the carrots in 1 tablespoon of oil and the honey. Season and roast on a baking tray in the oven for about 30 minutes, until tender.

Toss the carrots with the cooked lentils, garlic, soaked red onion and remaining olive oil. Rip the bread into small pieces and toast in the oven for 5 minutes or until crisp.

In a large bowl, gently mix together the bread, carrot and lentil mixture and the salad leaves. Check the seasoning. Transfer to a serving dish and crumble the goat's cheese over or drizzle with the dressing.

Franco's Italian Summer Pudding

Summer pudding is a classic and I don't like to mess around with it too much. In this version Franco Taruschio, who used to own the Walnut Tree in Abergavenny, adds mascarpone and Amaretto or grappa, which lifts it to another level.

Serves 8

750g strawberries, quartered, plus more to serve
250g raspberries, plus more to serve
2 tablespoons Amaretto or grappa
150g icing sugar
1kg stale white bread
150ml double cream
250g mascarpone
few drops of vanilla extract
100g amaretti biscuits, crushed

For the sauce:
100g strawberries
100g raspberries
60ml grappa

Blend all the ingredients for the sauce together until smooth, then push the sauce through a sieve with a spatula.

Mix the quartered strawberries and whole raspberries with the Amaretto or grappa and 100g of the icing sugar, and leave to macerate for at least 30 minutes.

Remove the crusts from the bread and slice 1cm thick. Line a pudding bowl with cling film. Dip the bread in the sauce, making sure it really soaks in, and use it to line the bowl, saving some for the lid.

Whisk together the cream, mascarpone, vanilla and remaining icing sugar until stiff, then fold in the crushed amaretti.

Drain the macerating berries and reserve their juices. Layer the berries and mascarpone mixture in the bread-lined bowl, first berries then mascarpone, finishing with the remaining berries. Cover with the bread for the lid and drizzle with the reserved macerating juices and any remaining sauce. Cover with cling film, put a plate or saucer on top of the pudding and press down, place a weight on top and refrigerate overnight.

To serve, turn out and garnish with berries.

Everyday

Indonesian Corn Fritters
Corn and Courgette Soup
Quesadillas
Baked Fennel and Spinach
Courgettes with Saffron and Pine Nuts
Tortilla Soup with Corn and Chard
Curried Courgette with Almond and Mint
Baked Squash, Corn and Goat's Cheese with a Pumpkin Seed Dressing
Quick Italian Leek Salad
Fennel, Feta and Radish Salad with Nigella and Dill
Chard, Mushroom and Walnut Tart
Salt Cod and Peppers
Tortilla Salad
Fish in a Bag with Fennel and Tamarind
Simply Cooked Chard with Lemon and Dried Chilli

Sunday

Fennel Salad with Avocado, Watercress, Red Pepper and Chorizo
Creamed Corn
Chermoulah Chicken
Chocolate Almond Cake with Raspberries

SEPTEMBER

Feast and be happy

As a vegetable grower, cook and occasional surfer, September is the best month of the year. Crops, particularly organic ones, tend to look their best and we have the satisfaction of harvesting the fruits of our summer labours, and seeing the bank balance restored to health. As we approach the equinox and the days rapidly draw in, a contented autumn melancholy settles over the farm. Planting and weeding are over and summer staff depart to college or Poland or both, leaving our more experienced permanent core to harvest for the vegetable boxes each week and start bringing the roots into store. Along with a good proportion of our staff, I am a surfer; with the water at its warmest and with the first of the big autumn swells arriving on empty beaches, the vegetables sometimes have to wait.

Bean time is lean time

For cooks, September is one of the few months we can actually enjoy those Elizabeth David-inspired Mediterranean recipes without trucking or flying produce in or burning fuel to heat a greenhouse closer to home. Tomatoes, basil, peppers, aubergines, cucumber and chillies are still cropping heavily from unheated tunnels, while outside all the summer salads are being joined by sweetcorn, squash, leeks, Savoys and the main crop of runner beans. The abundance is overwhelming and, unfortunately, the nation's kitchens are often full of home-grown produce. Everyone from the allotment keeper to the vegetable baron of the Fens has too much of the same stuff, particularly runner beans, explaining the vegetable trade adage that 'bean time is lean time'.

Sweetcorn

We start picking sweetcorn in France in July and are sometimes picking early UK crops that have been pushed on with crop covers in mid August, but September brings the best, heaviest crops from the main crop varieties with their longer, better-filled cobs. If you're still barbecuing, leave the husks on and soak in a bucket of water before cooking slowly on each side until the husks start to catch; peel back and eat with salt and pepper and a knob of butter, using the husk as a handle. If you tire of eating it on the cob, having boiled them it is easy to cut off the kernels, using them to make fritters (wonderful with a freshly made chilli and green herb salsa) or, as autumn advances, a chowder (don't use all the flour that American recipes call for). Jane often serves corn in the Field Kitchen mixed with chard or other greens

Riverford organic veg
+ lots MORE to your door
no potatoes

no potatoes
organic seasons

Riverford
organic seasons
push here to fold box

and always makes her Dev-Mex soup (with pumpkin and corn; the recipe is in our first cook book) for our Pumpkin Day in October.

Lazy man's passata

The tunnels are cropping so heavily it is inevitable that some of the fruit gets over-ripe and it's time to make batches of tomato sauce, oven-dried tomatoes and the occasional ratatouille. I am a lazy cook and have developed the ultimate low-labour tomato sauce: having gently fried a little garlic and chilli, I fill the saucepan with tomatoes, vine, calyx and all (the vine imparts considerable extra flavour), bring to the boil and then simmer to reduce (by about half, depending on the tomatoes). Put through a mouli or coarse sieve and season to make the best sauce for pasta, pizzas, etc. It freezes well in old yoghurt pots for the winter.

Enjoying the last of summer

With the nights drawing in and everyone getting back to a more routine existence, September marks the start of a return to comfort cooking: fritters, risotto and roasted and baked vegetables are back. Don't be too keen to turn your back on salads just yet; by the end of the month, with falling light levels, the sun-loving tomatoes and lettuce may not be quite at their best, but they are still way better than anything you are going to get through the winter, so relish them while you can. Perhaps add a bit more substance and a hint of autumn by combining your leaves with roast squash (coming into season at the end of the month), a few pumpkin seeds, fennel or grilled courgettes. Nothing from a jar can come close to a fresh salsa made with tomato, chilli, red onions (preferably marinated) and fresh green herbs (any mixture of coriander, flat-leaf parsley, basil, chives, chervil). It is great on fritters, with fish, with tortilla chips, with scrambled eggs. It is best fresh but even after a few days in the fridge way better than anything pasteurised, which will have killed the fresh herbs.

Quick and easy ideas
SWEETCORN

Sweetcorn salsa

Add cooked kernels to chopped tomato, red onion, chilli, red pepper and coriander. Season and add lime or lemon juice and olive oil.

Grilled cobs

Try blending roasted and peeled red pepper flesh with butter, lime juice and chilli, or mixing butter with lemon zest and a little curry powder. Toss grilled sweetcorn cobs in this spiced seasoned butter.

Sweetcorn chowder

Cook finely chopped bacon with chopped onion, diced red pepper and chilli in a little oil and butter in a large pan. Add finely diced potatoes and sweetcorn scraped from the cob and cook gently for 5 minutes. Cover with milk and simmer until the potatoes are about to fall apart. Cooked mussels or clams can be added at this stage, or finish the soup by adding good-quality smoked haddock and simmering for 10 more minutes.

Sweetcorn and chorizo salad

Slice cooked sweetcorn from the cob and mix with rocket, sliced cooked salad potatoes and tomatoes. Fry sliced chorizo in a little oil and toss through the salad with vinegar and seasoning.

EVERYDAY

Indonesian Corn Fritters

These are a really popular dish down at Riverford – everyone seems to have their own variation. The best way to get the kernels off the corn cob is to cut off the end to get a flat surface, then stand the cob on a chopping board. Using a small, serrated knife in a sawing action, cut off the kernels, working your way round the cob. The fritters can also be vegetarian – just substitute pieces of cooked aubergine for the prawns.

Serves 6

kernels from 3 cooked sweetcorn cobs
200g raw prawns, shelled, deveined and roughly chopped
2 tablespoons finely chopped celery
1 garlic clove, crushed
2 chillies, deseeded if preferred, finely chopped
1 bunch of spring onions, or 1 onion, finely chopped
2 tablespoons rice flour
2 eggs, beaten
1 teaspoon ground coriander
pinch of ground cumin
pinch of cayenne pepper
2 tablespoons chopped coriander
1 teaspoon salt
sunflower oil, for frying

Roughly chop the corn kernels and mix in a bowl with all the other ingredients except the oil until well combined.

Add a little oil to a non-stick pan. When hot, add spoonfuls of the fritter batter and cook a few at a time until golden brown and crisp on each side.

Corn and Courgette Soup

Riverford Cook Anna Colquhoun adapted this from a dish she used to make while working at Chez Panisse in San Francisco. Serve with a dollop of the herb and chilli butter in each bowl.

Serves 6

4 cooked sweetcorn cobs
2 sprigs of thyme
1 sprig of parsley
1 bay leaf
1 onion, thinly sliced
sea salt and freshly ground black pepper
2 tablespoons olive oil
2 courgettes, thinly sliced
30g unsalted butter, softened
1 teaspoon chopped parsley
1 teaspoon finely chopped chives
pinch of chilli flakes
drops of Tabasco, to taste
1 teaspoon lime or lemon juice

Cut the corn kernels from the cobs (see opposite). Place the cobs in a pan with 2 litres of water and the thyme, parsley and bay, bring to a boil and simmer for about 30 minutes, to make a stock.

In a large saucepan, cook the onion with a little salt in the olive oil for about 10 minutes. Add the corn kernels, season and cook for another 10 minutes. Add the courgettes and stir well. Add some of the strained corn stock until the vegetables are just covered, reserving the rest of it. Simmer the soup for about 10 minutes or until the courgettes are tender. Remove from the heat.

Blend the butter with the rest of the ingredients (or mash with a fork).

Blend the soup in batches until smooth, then pass through a sieve. Add more stock if required, and season. Divide between 6 soup bowls and top each one with a spoonful of the flavoured butter.

Quesadillas

Corn tortillas are easy to find nowadays in most food shops but the best ones can be purchased from the Cool Chile Co. by mail order. The quesadillas must be fried until crispy on both sides, and it doesn't matter if some of the filling falls out when you turn them over. This is great party food.

Serves 4

For the filling:
½ red onion, chopped
2 teaspoons sugar
2 teaspoons balsamic vinegar
1 cooked chicken breast, chopped
100g cooked sweetcorn, cut from the cob
1 red chilli, deseeded if preferred, chopped
1 tablespoon chopped coriander
½ tablespoon chopped mint
50g Gruyère cheese, grated
50g feta cheese, crumbled
pinch of smoked paprika
sea salt and freshly ground black pepper

To assemble:
2 tablespoons olive oil
30g unsalted butter
6–8 corn tortillas

Soak the red onion in the sugar and vinegar for 30 minutes. Mix together all the filling ingredients and season well. Melt half the oil and butter in a non-stick pan.

Put a little of the filling to one side of a tortilla, and fold over the other half to make a pasty shape. Place in the hot butter and oil, hold down with a spatula and reduce the heat. When the base is crisp, carefully turn over (don't worry, some filling always spills out) and crisp up the other side. Remove to kitchen paper to drain and repeat with the rest of the tortillas, using the rest of the oil and butter when needed. If you fancy your chances, do two at once! Cut each quesadilla in half and serve.

Baked Fennel and Spinach

This is a really popular dish at the Field Kitchen. It was actually born out of a shortage when we were making a fennel gratin – we added spinach and this was the result. I take off the fennel fronds (otherwise they'll burn) and remove the tough outer skin, but, with tender English fennel, I leave in the core – just be sure to cook the fennel until really softened.

Serves 6

2 fennel bulbs
2 tablespoons olive oil
2 garlic cloves, crushed
1 teaspoon ground fennel seeds
400g spinach, washed and stalks removed
sea salt and freshly ground black pepper
100ml double cream
1 tablespoon finely grated Parmesan cheese
1 tablespoon soft breadcrumbs
zest of 1 unwaxed lemon
1 tablespoon chopped parsley

Preheat the oven to 180°C/Gas Mark 4.

Trim the fennel and cut into thin wedges. Cook it in the hot oil in a sauté pan until brown, then reduce the heat and cook slowly for 15 minutes, adding a little water if it's sticking to the pan. Add the garlic and ground fennel seeds and cook for 5 more minutes.

Blanch the spinach in boiling salted water for 2 minutes, drain and refresh in cold water. Squeeze out the excess water and chop roughly. Add to the braised fennel with the cream, increase the heat, mix and season well.

Transfer to a baking dish. Mix together the Parmesan, breadcrumbs, lemon zest and parsley and scatter over the fennel and spinach. Bake in the oven for 15 minutes.

Courgettes with Saffron and Pine Nuts

During a quick road stop at a small restaurant outside Florence, I had an unexpectedly brilliant and simple meal. Strips of courgette were cooked gently with saffron and served with spinach and ricotta ravioli. This is a re-creation of that sauce. Try not to crowd the courgettes in the pan, otherwise they'll sweat; cook them in batches if necessary instead. Serve with a good-quality ready-made ravioli for a great supper dish, or you could eat it with plain pasta. It would also be a lovely side dish with lamb.

Serves 4

50g raisins
pinch of saffron
700g courgettes
1 onion, thinly sliced
3 tablespoons olive oil
2 tablespoons pine nuts, lightly toasted
sea salt and freshly ground black pepper

About 30 minutes before assembling the dish, put the raisins and saffron in 2 small bowls. Add 3 tablespoons boiling water to the saffron, and cover the raisins in hot water.

Cut the courgettes into quarters lengthways. Remove any spongy seeds, then cut each quarter again in half lengthways.

Cook the onion slowly in the olive oil for about 20 minutes, until golden. Remove from the heat. Drain the oil from the onions, set the onions aside and return the oil to the pan. Increase the heat and, when the oil is hot, add the courgettes and cook for about 5 minutes until just tender. Return the onion, add the saffron water, the drained raisins and the pine nuts. Cook for a few minutes until the water has almost evaporated. Season.

Tortilla Soup with Corn and Chard

Every September we hold a Mexican evening at the Field Kitchen to celebrate the corn, chillies and tomatoes that are all in season. Mexican cuisine can be quite complex, with a huge number of chilli varieties to be roasted, smoked and ground. However, this tortilla soup is relatively simple and looks great. Serve as a fresh starter or light lunch.

Serves 6

6 corn tortillas
4 tablespoons olive oil
4 large chillies
1 litre chicken stock, plus more if needed
kernels from 2 sweetcorn cobs
1 onion, chopped
2 red chillies, deseeded if preferred, sliced
2 garlic cloves, crushed
1 sprig of thyme
1 teaspoon ground cumin
1 teaspoon smoked paprika
½ teaspoon ground cinnamon
400g tinned chopped tomatoes
1 tablespoon honey
1 cooked chicken, meat removed from the carcass and shredded,
    or 4 cooked chicken breasts, shredded
400g chard, stems removed, leaves shredded
sea salt and freshly ground black pepper
juice of 1 lime
2 avocados, chopped
handful of coriander leaves

Preheat the oven to 180°C/Gas Mark 4. Cut the tortillas into 1cm–wide strips. Toss in half the olive oil and bake in the oven for about 10 minutes until golden and crisp. Set aside.

Remove the seeds from the large chillies, chop and simmer in a pot with the chicken stock for 15 minutes.

While the chillies are simmering, cook the corn kernels in the remaining oil over a high heat so they brown slightly, stirring constantly. Add the onion, red chillies, garlic and thyme, and cook for 5 minutes. Add the spices and mix well, then add the tomatoes and bring to a simmer.

Blend together the chicken stock and chillies and add to the vegetables. Return to a simmer, adding the honey, shredded chicken and chard. Cook for another 15 minutes, check the seasoning and let down with more chicken stock if required. Finish with lime juice. To serve, divide the tortilla pieces between 6 warmed bowls along with the avocado. Ladle the soup over the tortillas and sprinkle with coriander leaves.

Curried Courgette with Almond and Mint

Based on a recipe in Patricia Wells' *The Paris Cookbook*, this is a great, simple recipe for when you have plenty of courgettes to use up. For a quick recipe like this, it's fine to use a shop-bought curry powder rather than mixing your own spices. Just be sure that it's freshly opened, as spices quickly lose their flavour. Serve with basmati rice for a simple meal, or as a side dish with Indian food.

Serves 4

600g courgettes, trimmed, cut in half and sliced lengthways
100g flaked almonds
2 teaspoons good-quality curry powder
sea salt and freshly ground black pepper
2 tablespoons extra virgin olive oil
a few mint leaves, cut into fine ribbons

Combine the courgettes, almonds, curry, salt and pepper in a bowl. Cover and set aside for 15 minutes. In a large frying pan, heat the oil over a high heat until hot. Transfer the courgette mixture to the pan and cook for about 5 minutes until golden. Taste for seasoning and add the mint.

Baked Squash, Corn and Goat's Cheese with a Pumpkin Seed Dressing

This is a vegetarian take on the Mexican dish *queso fundido*. There are many varieties of squash to choose from at this time of year – butternut works well for this recipe, as does onion squash. I also think Kabacha and Crown Prince are very good. The dressing should be used when freshly made – it loses its flavour after a day in the fridge. This is great served with warmed corn tortillas.

Serves 4–6

1 squash (about 1kg butternut or onion), peeled and deseeded
1 tablespoon olive oil
sea salt and freshly ground black pepper
3 sweetcorn cobs
2 garlic cloves, very finely chopped
2 red chillies, deseeded if preferred, finely chopped
200g goat's cheese, crumbled or chopped
juice of 1 lime
handful of chopped coriander

For the pumpkin seed dressing:
80g pumpkin seeds
2 garlic cloves, crushed
2 tomatoes (green if possible, but not to worry!)
2 green lettuce leaves, chopped (Romaine or Cos)
1 tablespoon chopped coriander
2 green chillies, deseeded if preferred, roughly chopped
2 tablespoons olive oil

Preheat the oven to 190°C/Gas Mark 5. Chop the squash into 1–2cm chunks. Toss in the olive oil, season and roast in the oven for about 30 minutes, until starting to brown and just cooked through.

While the squash is cooking, cook the corn in boiling water for about 10 minutes. Cool and cut the kernels from the cob (see page 232).

Toss the squash with the garlic, chillies and corn. Transfer to an ovenproof serving dish and return to the oven for another 5 minutes.

Make the pumpkin seed dressing by dry-frying the seeds over a medium heat for 5 minutes until they are toasted and have popped. When cool, blend in a liquidiser with all the other dressing ingredients, season and add a little water to make a pouring consistency.

Fold the goat's cheese into the squash and corn mix and return to the oven for another 10 minutes, or until the cheese is hot.

To serve, squeeze the lime juice over, drizzle with the pumpkin seed dressing and sprinkle with coriander.

Quick Italian Leek Salad

The first leeks of the year deserve some special attention. This is the perfect recipe for them – they are dressed very simply, allowing them to show off all their flavour.

Serves 4

3 tablespoons olive oil
1 tablespoon balsamic vinegar
½ red onion (or shallot), finely chopped
10 basil leaves, shredded
pinch of caster sugar
sea salt and freshly ground black pepper
4–6 leeks
1 tablespoon chopped parsley
shavings of Parmesan cheese, to serve

Mix the oil, vinegar, onion, basil and sugar together and season to make the dressing.

Trim the leeks, cut down the centre lengthways, then wash well. Slice diagonally into 3–4cm pieces. Blanch in boiling salted water for about 3 minutes. Drain well and place in a shallow serving dish, drizzle with the dressing and mix well. This can be served now while it's warm, topped with the parsley and Parmesan, or later, chilled.

Fennel, Feta and Radish Salad with Nigella and Dill

Riverford Cook Francesca Melman, who worked with me for a while in the early days of the River Café, has given us this fresh and stunning dish. A potato peeler can work just as well as a mandolin to shave the radishes and fennel.

Serves 4

1 fennel bulb, shaved thinly on a mandolin
½ cucumber, deseeded, shaved thinly on a mandolin
6 radishes, shaved thinly on a mandolin
125g feta cheese, cubed
juice of 1 lemon
2 tablespoons olive oil
sea salt and freshly ground black pepper
sprinkling of nigella seeds
2 sprigs of dill, chopped

Mix the shaved fennel, cucumber and radishes with the feta. Dress with the lemon and olive oil. Season with salt and pepper. Place on a serving dish and sprinkle with the nigella seeds and dill.

Chard, Mushroom and Walnut Tart

Sometimes it's quite challenging to come up with new, specifically vegetarian options at the Field Kitchen. The other vegetable dishes are often quite complex themselves and can steal the limelight from a main dish. This tart, however, is packed with flavour and impossible to overshadow. You can bake the filling in a gratin dish on its own, and can substitute spinach for chard at other times of year.

Serves 6

For the shortcrust pastry:
175g plain flour, plus more to dust
1 teaspoon caster sugar
pinch of salt
125g cold unsalted butter, cut into knobs

For the filling:
1 onion, finely chopped
30g unsalted butter
1 tablespoon olive oil
300g mushrooms, very finely sliced
1 teaspoon thyme leaves
1 garlic clove, crushed
300g chard
sea salt and freshly ground black pepper
50g walnuts, toasted
100ml double cream
1 egg yolk
1 tablespoon finely grated Parmesan cheese

For the pastry, put the flour, sugar and salt in a food processor and pulse briefly to mix. Add the butter and pulse until the mixture resembles fine breadcrumbs. Transfer to a bowl and stir in enough cold water (about 3 tablespoons) to make a dough. Wrap in cling film and chill for at least 30 minutes. Preheat the oven to 180°C/Gas Mark 4.

Roll out the pastry on a lightly floured surface and use it to line a 22cm loose-bottomed flan tin. Cover the base and sides with baking parchment and fill with baking beans or raw rice. Bake for 15–20 minutes, removing the paper and beans for the last 5 minutes, until golden brown. Leave to cool.

Preheat the oven once more to 180°C/Gas Mark 4. Cook the onion slowly in the butter and oil for 5 minutes. Add the mushrooms, thyme and garlic and cook for 10 more minutes.

While the mushrooms are cooking, wash the chard and remove the stalks, then blanch the leaves in boiling salted water for 1 minute. Drain, refresh with cold water and squeeze out the excess moisture. Coarsely chop, season well, add to the cooked mushrooms and mix well. Braise together for 5 minutes more. Season and remove from the heat.

Chop the walnuts roughly and add to the mushrooms with the cream. Cook all together for 10 minutes, then cool.

Mix in the egg yolk and transfer the filling to the pastry case. Sprinkle with the Parmesan and bake for about 30 minutes until set.

Salt Cod and Peppers

This is based on a Jamaican dish – salt cod and ackee. Ackee is a creamy yellow fruit; it's hard to find fresh here but you can sometimes get tinned. Ripe avocado is a good substitute. This is a great way to use up spare peppers, but try to find a good Caribbean pepper sauce for the best flavour. You can serve this with rice and avocado, but it's also really good with poached or scrambled eggs.

Serves 6

500g salt cod
2 onions, finely sliced
2 tablespoons olive oil
sea salt and freshly ground black pepper
1 red pepper, deseeded and finely sliced
1 yellow pepper, deseeded and finely sliced
2 garlic cloves, crushed
2 hot chillies, deseeded if preferred, chopped
200g fresh or tinned tomatoes, roughly chopped
juice of 1 lime
1 tablespoon chopped coriander
hot pepper sauce, to taste

Soak the salt cod in plenty of cold water for 24 hours, changing the water a few times.

Simmer in fresh water for 20–30 minutes until soft and the flesh is falling from the bone. Drain and flake the cod from the bone and skin. Set aside.

In a frying pan, cook the onions in the olive oil with a little salt for about 10 minutes until soft, then add the peppers and cook for a further 15 minutes, stirring occasionally. Now add the garlic and chillies and cook for a minute before adding the tomatoes. Increase the heat and cook the mixture for a further 10 minutes. Gently mix in the flakes of cod and reduce the heat to warm through. Finish with the lime juice, coriander and some hot pepper sauce to taste.

Tortilla Salad

Introducing crispy tortilla strips gives this quick and simple salad an interesting edge. Daikon is a kind of white radish – you could use normal radishes if they're easier to get hold of.

Serves 4

2 large or 6 small corn tortillas
2 tablespoons sunflower oil
1 red pepper, deseeded and thinly sliced
1 yellow pepper, deseeded and thinly sliced
1 carrot, peeled and cut into matchsticks, or 6 radishes, sliced
3 chillies, deseeded if preferred, finely chopped
½ daikon, peeled and cut into matchsticks (optional)
2 tablespoons chopped coriander
100g mizuna, rocket or mixed salad leaves
2 tablespoons pumpkin seeds

For the dressing:
3 tablespoons sunflower oil
2 tablespoons rice wine vinegar
2 teaspoons caster sugar
pinch of cayenne pepper
1 tablespoon finely chopped shallots or salad onions
1 garlic clove, crushed
pinch of salt

Cut the tortillas into halves, then into thin strips. Gently fry them in batches in the sunflower oil until lightly coloured and crispy. Drain and cool on kitchen paper.

In a bowl, mix together the peppers, carrot, chillies, daikon (if using) and coriander.

Whisk together the dressing ingredients and toss with the mizuna or rocket.

Add the crispy tortilla strips and pumpkin seeds to the salad just before serving, add the dressing and toss gently.

Fish in a Bag with Fennel and Tamarind

Cooking fish 'al cartoccio' (in a bag) is very quick and the juices mix together for a ready-made sauce. At La Petite Maison in London, I ate a similar fish dish that used tamarind. It was so good that we experimented and came up with this. Serve with braised spinach and lentils.

Serves 4

1 tablespoon olive oil
1 red onion, very finely sliced
2 fennel bulbs, trimmed and very finely sliced
sea salt and freshly ground black pepper
4 x 150–175g sea bass fillets (or sea bream, halibut or gurnard)
4 teaspoons tamarind paste
cayenne pepper
splash of white wine
4 knobs of unsalted butter

Preheat the oven to 200°C/Gas Mark 6.

Lay out 4 pieces of baking parchment, each about 30cm x 30cm, on a work surface. In the centre of each, smear a little olive oil. Mix together the onion and fennel, and season.

Divide half the fennel mixture between the 4 portions. Place a piece of fish on top and spread each with the tamarind. Season with salt and cayenne pepper and top with the remaining fennel and onion.

Add a little white wine and a knob of butter to each and fold over the paper to make a parcel, rolling up the edges to form a pouch. To make sure the edges are sealed, the odd staple helps.

Place the parcels on a baking tray and bake in the hot oven for 10 minutes. Allow to sit for 5 minutes before opening to serve.

Simply Cooked Chard with Lemon and Dried Chilli

Chard stalks are perfectly edible and shouldn't be discarded when you use the leaves. They do, however, need to be cooked separately, as they take longer to soften. When rainbow chard is in season this dish will look pretty with the many-coloured stems.

Serves 4–6

300–400g chard
2 tablespoons olive oil
sea salt and freshly ground black pepper
pinch of dried chilli, or to taste
juice of ½ lemon
extra virgin olive oil, to serve

Remove the chard leaves from the stems. Blanch the stalks in boiling salted water for 3–4 minutes, then drain and refresh in cold water.

Wash the leaves, drain and cut into rough strips. Sauté in the olive oil for about 5 minutes, covered, until the leaves are tender. Uncover, add the stalks and boil away any excess water. Season, add chilli to taste, a squeeze of lemon juice and a splash of extra virgin olive oil.

SUNDAY

Fennel Salad with Avocado, Watercress, Red Pepper and Chorizo

The oil that comes out of good-quality cooking chorizo when fried slowly has such a good flavour, it's a shame to waste it. Here it is put to good use in the dressing for this fresh autumn salad. You can make a vegetarian version as well, though – just leave out the chorizo – the remaining salad ingredients are still stunning. Soaking the shaved fennel in iced water is a good trick to help it crisp up.

Serves 4

1 large fennel bulb
2 oranges, segmented
2 avocados, peeled and sliced
1 bunch of watercress, washed and trimmed
2 tablespoons toasted and chopped unsalted pistachios

For the dressing:
200g spicy cooking chorizo, skinned and cut into small pieces
finely grated zest and juice of 1 orange
2 tablespoons sherry vinegar
2 tablespoons extra virgin olive oil
100g piquillo peppers (or a jar of other roasted, skinned peppers), finely chopped
sea salt and freshly ground black pepper

Shave the fennel very finely on a mandolin (or with a sharp knife). Place in the fridge in some iced water to crisp.

For the dressing, dry-fry the chorizo in a pan for about 10 minutes until its oil runs out and the chorizo is cooked. Cool for 5 minutes, then mix with the orange zest and juice, vinegar, oil and peppers to make the dressing. Season well.

In a large bowl, mix the orange segments, avocado and watercress. Drain and dry the fennel and combine it with the other salad ingredients. Drizzle with the dressing and sprinkle with pistachios.

Creamed Corn

This is probably the most enquired about dish at the Field Kitchen. It is based on a recipe by Sean Moran, whose restaurant, Sean's Panorama, overlooks Bondi Beach in Sydney. His food is produce-led – much of it coming from his own smallholding. The key to the flavour of this dish is allowing the corn to caramelise. You don't have to cream the corn at the end, you could serve with all the kernels still whole. You can also add chopped chard or spinach at the end of cooking.

Serves 4–6

1 large onion, finely chopped
1 teaspoon thyme leaves
1 red chilli, deseeded if preferred, chopped
2 garlic cloves, finely chopped
1 tablespoon olive oil
50g butter
kernels from 4 sweetcorn cobs
½ teaspoon cumin seeds, ground
100ml dry white wine
300ml chicken stock
sea salt and freshly ground black pepper

In a heavy-based pan over a moderate heat, cook the onion, thyme, chilli and garlic in the oil and butter for 5 minutes until lightly caramelised.

Add the corn kernels and cumin and cook for 10 minutes, stirring constantly. The corn will start to catch on the bottom of the pan, but you do want it to brown slightly.

Deglaze with the wine and stock, then bring to a steady simmer and cook for about 20 minutes or until the corn is tender.

Remove from the heat and allow to cool slightly.

Set aside a large spoonful of corn, then blend the remaining corn in a food processor, or with a stick blender, for a couple of minutes. Pass through a sieve, then return the reserved spoonful of corn and season well to taste.

Chermoulah Chicken

I don't think it's always essential to toast and grind your own spices, but it is important for a marinade of this kind. The exception is cumin – which tastes so much better if you prepare it yourself that it's always worth the extra effort. Whole spices lose their flavour less quickly than pre-ground spices, so if your spices are a bit old it can be best to roast and grind from scratch rather than use powdered. You can also use the chermoulah marinade on lamb leg steaks or fish. You could even use it with root vegetables before roasting.

Serves 4

2 chicken breasts
2–4 boneless chicken thighs
sea salt and freshly ground black pepper

For the chermoulah:
pinch of saffron
2 teaspoons cumin seeds
1 teaspoon coriander seeds
1 teaspoon fennel seeds
juice of 1 lemon
1 tablespoon red wine vinegar
1 garlic clove, crushed
1 chilli, deseeded if preferred, finely chopped
1 teaspoon brown sugar
pinch of cinnamon
2 teaspoons sweet paprika
2 tablespoons olive oil
1 tablespoon chopped coriander

First prepare the chermoulah. Soak the saffron in 2 tablespoons hot water for 20 minutes. Meanwhile, dry-fry the cumin, coriander and fennel seeds until golden and fragrant, then pound them to a powder in a mortar and pestle or spice grinder. Mix the saffron, its water and the ground seeds with all the other chermoulah ingredients.

Toss the chicken pieces through the chermoulah and leave, covered, for at least 1 hour. Preheat the oven to 180°C/Gas Mark 4. In a hot griddle pan, grill each chicken piece for a few minutes on each side until browned.

When all the pieces are browned, transfer to an ovenproof dish, season with salt and pepper and cook in the oven for 10 minutes, until firm to the touch and cooked through. Serve.

Chocolate Almond Cake with Raspberries

In the Field Kitchen we incorporate lovely autumn raspberries into this classic Elizabeth David chocolate cake – they are added just before cooking and make it closer to a pudding than a cake. It also works well with redcurrants. Serve with crème fraîche. This is a gluten-free pudding.

Serves 10

200g unsalted butter, softened, plus more for the tin
250g good-quality dark chocolate
2 tablespoons brandy
2 tablespoons strong brewed coffee
250g caster sugar
250g ground almonds
125g rice flour
6 eggs, separated
250g raspberries

Preheat the oven to 160°C/Gas Mark 3. Butter a 20cm cake tin and line the base with baking parchment.

Place the chocolate, brandy, coffee and butter in a bowl placed over a saucepan of simmering water (don't let the base of the bowl touch the water). When melted, stir in the sugar, ground almonds and rice flour. Beat in the egg yolks. Whisk the egg whites to stiff peaks and fold in 1 tablespoon to loosen the mixture, then fold in all the rest. Fold in the raspberries.

Empty the batter into the prepared tin and bake for 45 minutes.

Everyday

Oriental Salad with Aubergines
Spiced Aubergine and Tomato
Aubergine Sarnies
Roasted Cauliflower with Chorizo, Red Pepper and Capers
Quick Mouclade of Mussels
Pork Fillet with Celery, Apples and Mustard
Grilled Leeks with Quick Romesco Sauce
Grilled Radicchio with Marjoram and Mozzarella
Mackerel Escabeche
Squash Gnudi
Pan-fried Chicken Livers with Sage and Radicchio
Spiced Turnip, Potato and Squash Gratin

Sunday

Pot-roasted Guineafowl with Coppa, Sage and Rosemary
Warm Salad of Grilled Leeks, Fennel and Roasted Romanesco
Swiss Chard, Squash and Blue Cheese Torte
Plum, Blackberry (or Blueberry) and Amaretti Crumble

OCTOBER

Time to preserve

The abundance of September and October can be overwhelming and, with winter approaching, the desire to preserve that abundance for the leaner times to come can be obsessive. As the first frosts threaten, I cannot bear to see the small globe artichokes going to waste and I feel compelled to turn my kitchen into a factory devoted to preserving them in wine vinegar, spices and olive oil. For others it is making chutney, freezing down sweetcorn or beans, jamming the last of the autumn raspberries, or drying apples, chillies and mushrooms in the airing cupboard. The rationalists in the house may point out that the time and cost of materials involved make this a wholly senseless process better done by machines, at scale, in a distant factory where labour is cheap and a consistent product can be guaranteed. Economic rationalism makes for a sad home though – there are few things more satisfying and reassuring than entering winter with a cupboard full of preserves.

Bring in the squash

We watch the weather forecast and wait until the first frost threatens (normally in early October) before harvesting the squash and pumpkins; even in the south we are on the climatic extreme for these tender cucurbits, so they need every last day of sunshine to develop their full flavour and lose the wet soapiness of under-ripe fruit. The buff-coloured butternut squash dominates the market, perhaps because it can be peeled with relative ease (and a good vegetable peeler). When I first grew butternut twenty years ago its flavour could be excellent. As plant breeders have tamed the crop, much of the flavour has been lost in hybrids bred for early ripening, yield and uniform size. As a farmer and cook, I prefer the large, blue-grey Crown Prince, provided you have a sharp knife and strong hand for the peeling. If you are a gardener you will find it is also a reliable and heavy cropper, and it is easily the best keeper. Squash like to be warm and dry (a kitchen shelf is ideal) and should never be put in the fridge (unless they have been cut and you need to preserve a half for future use, in which case they should keep for 7–10 days). In the warm, a well-ripened, whole butternut should keep for a month or two. Crown Prince can keep right through to the spring in good conditions.

Autumn salads

Lettuces love sunshine. With light levels dropping, they lose their crunch and sweetness, become susceptible to disease and tend not to keep. If your appetite for green salads extends beyond summer, there are lots of alternative leaves that last well up to Christmas, tolerating a bit of frost and less light. Some can

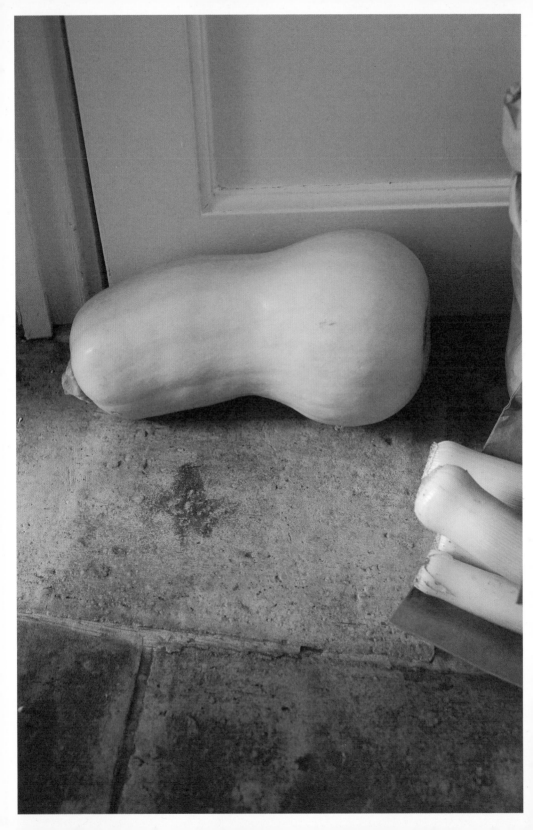

survive the winter: piquant brassicas (ranging from the mild mizunas and baby pak choy, through the peppery rocket to the fiery mustards); earthy baby spinach, chard and beet leaves; hot American landcress (three times as strong as watercress); succulent claytonia or miner's lettuce, mild and subtle mâche (lamb's lettuce), loved on the Continent; intensely bitter dandelion-relatives radicchio, escarole, frisée and endive. We are able to harvest a good range of leaves outside through to late November before moving into our tunnels. If you are prepared to pick individual leaves selectively and like a peppery salad, it is possible to pick your own salad leaves from a garden right through a mild winter.

Quick and easy ideas
SQUASH

Spicy roast squash

Toss cubes of squash or pumpkin in a little oil. Season and roast in a medium oven until tender. Mix Parmesan cheese and breadcrumbs with chopped garlic, chilli and rosemary. Sprinkle over the squash. Return to the oven until browned.

Roast squash and quinoa salad

Toss roasted squash cubes with cooked quinoa, chopped red onion, toasted walnuts, crumbled feta and chopped cooked greens (spinach, chard or kale would be good). Dress with balsamic vinegar and olive oil. Season well. Pumpkin oil drizzled over is a good addition; topping with crispy fried sage is even better.

Quick squash lasagne

Roast cubes of squash in a medium oven with sage and chilli. Layer with lasagne sheets (ones that do not need pre-cooking) and a mixture of cheeses, such as mozzarella, ricotta, Fontina and Parmesan. Bake in the oven. Or try layering with prosciutto and adding a little blue cheese and chopped spinach to the cheeses.

Squash with watercress and blue cheese

Roast cubes of squash in a medium oven until almost tender. Sprinkle with garlic, chilli and rosemary and return to the oven for 5 more minutes. Mix with watercress and crumble some blue cheese on top.

EVERYDAY

Oriental Salad with Aubergines

When I worked at Leilei restaurant in Honiara in the Solomon Islands, this appeared regularly on the menu. Fresh vegetables were sometimes scarce, due to the political turmoil at the time, but there were usually aubergines in the market. Aubergines are perfect for this dish, as their sponge-like texture soaks up all the favours of the sauce. The salad can be eaten on its own or with grilled meat or fish. It's based on a recipe by a great Aussie chef, Christine Manfield, from her book *Spice*.

Serves 4–6

2 large aubergines
sea salt
3 tablespoons sunflower oil
3 small dried chillies, stalks removed, deseeded if preferred
½ teaspoon fennel seeds
½ teaspoon Sichuan peppercorns
3 garlic cloves, crushed
2cm piece fresh root ginger, finely chopped
2 red chillies, deseeded if preferred, finely chopped
2 tablespoons dry sherry
2 tablespoons rice vinegar
3 tablespoons soy sauce
1 tablespoon caster sugar
1 teaspoon sesame oil
4 spring onions, chopped
2 tablespoons chopped coriander

Preheat the oven to 180°C/Gas Mark 4.

Cut the aubergines into 2cm cubes, sprinkle with salt and leave them for 20 minutes on a piece of kitchen towel. Pat them dry, toss them in a little of the sunflower oil and roast in the oven for about 20 minutes until just cooked.

Grind the dried chillies, fennel seeds and Sichuan peppercorns in a mortar and pestle or spice grinder.

Add the rest of the sunflower oil to a wok and stir-fry the garlic, ginger and fresh chillies for a few minutes with the ground spices.

Add the aubergine, mix together well and quickly follow with the sherry, rice vinegar, soy sauce, 2 tablespoons of water and the sugar. Simmer for 5 minutes.

Remove from the heat before adding the rest of the ingredients.

Spiced Aubergine and Tomato

This is similar to the famous Turkish dish imam bayildi ('the imam fainted'). It's quick to make and good served hot or cold with grilled lamb, with goat's cheese crumbled over, or as part of a mezze platter.

Serves 4

3 tablespoons olive oil
1 aubergine, cut into 1cm cubes
3 garlic cloves, thinly sliced
400g tin chopped tomatoes
1 teaspoon caster sugar
pinch of ground allspice
pinch of cayenne pepper
splash of balsamic vinegar
sea salt and freshly ground black pepper
handful of chopped coriander, mint or parsley

In a large frying pan, heat the oil and sauté the aubergine until golden brown and tender. Remove with a slotted spoon on to kitchen roll to remove excess oil. Add the garlic to the remaining oil in the pan. Cook for a few minutes on a low heat, until the garlic is cooked but not browned. Add the tomatoes with the sugar, allspice and cayenne pepper.

Increase the heat and reduce the tomato down for about 10 minutes until very thick. Return the aubergine to the pan. Heat through gently and add the balsamic vinegar. Season well. Finish with the herbs.

Aubergine Sarnies

These are really good served as a vegetarian starter, but also make a great accompaniment to grilled lamb or fish. Serve with Basic Tomato Sauce (see page 207) and a few pieces of grilled red pepper.

Serves 4 as a starter

1 aubergine
100g ground almonds
70g finely grated Parmesan cheese
3 eggs, beaten
1 garlic clove, crushed
1 tablespoon chopped parsley
½ tablespoon chopped mint
sea salt and freshly ground black pepper
olive oil, for frying

Preheat the oven to 180°C/Gas Mark 4.

Thinly slice the aubergine into rounds about 5mm thick. Mix the rest of the ingredients, except the oil, together to make a paste and season well.

Spread the paste about 5mm thick on half the aubergine slices and top with the rest, pressing down firmly.

In an ovenproof, preferably non-stick frying pan, heat up a few tablespoons of olive oil and fry the aubergine sarnies until golden brown on each side. Finish in the oven for 5 minutes.

Roasted Cauliflower with Chorizo, Red Pepper and Capers

In this recipe the cauliflower is roasted with the chorizo, and soaks up some of its spicy, red oil. The sweet red pepper and sharp capers balance out the dish perfectly. It works well served with Chermoulah Chicken (see page 254), fish or grilled scallops.

Serves 4–6

1 tablespoon capers
3 red peppers
sea salt and freshly ground black pepper
200g cooking chorizo, skinned and chopped
1 large or 2 small cauliflowers, broken into florets
1 tablespoon sherry vinegar (or wine vinegar)
sprinkling of chopped parsley or mint leaves

Preheat the oven to 180°C/Gas Mark 4.

Place the capers in a small bowl, cover with water and leave to soak for 20 minutes. Squeeze out the excess water, and chop.

Meanwhile, grill or roast the red peppers to blacken the skin. Then place in a bowl while hot, cover with cling film and allow to sweat. When cool, remove the skins and seeds. Chop the flesh roughly and season well.

Dry-fry the chorizo in a pan until the oil runs out and the chorizo is cooked.

Place the cauliflower on a baking tray. Toss with the chorizo and its oil, the red peppers and capers. Season well and roast for 15–20 minutes.

Remove from the oven and sprinkle with the vinegar and herbs.

Quick Mouclade of Mussels

I think this is an overlooked mussel dish that deserves more recognition. The sauce, combining leeks, mussels and curry, is the sort that makes you want to pick up the bowl and down the lot!

Serves 4

2kg mussels in their shells
4 leeks, finely chopped
2 garlic cloves, crushed
pinch of saffron
1 teaspoon good-quality curry powder
1 tablespoon olive oil
15g unsalted butter
250ml dry cider
1 egg yolk
250ml double cream
1 teaspoon cornflour
handful of chopped parsley

Clean the mussels in cold water, remove their beards and discard any that are open.

In a large pan, cook the leeks, garlic, saffron and curry powder in the oil and butter for about 10 minutes. Add the cider, bring to a boil and throw in the mussels. Cover, and leave on a high heat until the mussels start to open. Strain the mussels and keep warm.

Return the cooking liquor to the pan and reduce by half over a high heat. Whisk the egg yolk with the cream and cornflour, then add the mixture slowly to the hot sauce, whisking all the time. The sauce should thicken. Pour over the mussels and sprinkle with parsley. Warn your diners to discard any mussels that remain shut.

Pork Fillet with Celery, Apples and Mustard

Chloe Hill, who helps us out in the Field Kitchen at outdoor catering events, gave me the idea for this recipe. It's a great way to use up celery, but you could use leeks instead. Be careful not to overcook the pork fillet.

Serves 4

1 celery heart and leaves
15g unsalted butter
1 tablespoon olive oil
1 pork fillet, about 420g, trimmed
sea salt and freshly ground black pepper
1 red onion, chopped
1 garlic clove, crushed
1 sprig of thyme
2 teaspoons wholegrain mustard
1 teaspoon Dijon mustard
150ml cider
2 eating apples
150ml chicken stock
1 tablespoon crème fraîche
1 tablespoon chopped parsley

Remove the leaves from the celery heart, chop and set aside. Cut the celery sticks into thin batons.

Heat the butter and oil in a large frying pan. Add the pork fillet. Season well and brown. Add the onion and celery batons and cook over a medium heat with the pork, turning regularly, for about 10 minutes. Add the garlic and thyme. Cook for another minute before adding the mustards and cider. Cook over a gentle heat for another 10 minutes; the pork should now be firmer. Remove the pork from the pan and cover to rest in a warm place. Peel the apples and cut them into wedges.

Increase the heat and add the stock and apple wedges. Reduce the sauce until it is of a coating consistency before whisking in the crème fraîche and parsley.

Slice the pork fillet, return to the sauce and serve topped with shredded celery leaves.

Grilled Leeks with Quick Romesco Sauce

Romesco sauce can seem like a bit of a faff to make, but it really is worth the effort. This simplified method should take out some of the pain, without losing any of the flavour. The sauce is good with the leeks, but you can also use it, earlier in the year, with grilled spring onions, or with fish, chicken or lamb.

Serves 4

12 small leeks
sea salt and freshly ground black pepper
1 teaspoon olive oil

For the sauce:
3 tomatoes
8 garlic cloves, unpeeled
200ml extra virgin olive oil
1 slice stale white bread, torn into smaller pieces
2 tablespoons flaked almonds
2 tablespoons blanched hazelnuts
200g piquillo peppers (or a jar of other roasted, skinned peppers)
2 red chillies, deseeded if preferred
1 teaspoon paprika
75ml sherry vinegar

Preheat the oven to 180°C/Gas Mark 4.

First make the sauce. Roast the tomatoes and garlic for 20 minutes. Peel the garlic and place the flesh in a food processor with the tomatoes. Put 2 tablespoons of the olive oil in a pan, add the white bread, almonds and hazelnuts and place over a medium heat until lightly toasted. Add to the tomatoes with the peppers, chillies and paprika. Blitz slowly, adding the rest of the oil and the vinegar. Check the seasoning.

Trim the leeks, then wash and blanch in boiling salted water for 5 minutes. Drain, cool and cut them in half lengthways. Toss in the olive oil. Season and grill on a hot griddle for a minute on each side. Remove and set aside.

Serve drizzled with the romesco sauce.

Grilled Radicchio with Marjoram and Mozzarella

Radicchio is an underused vegetable. I think people are put off by its bitterness, but as long as it is used in a well-balanced dish, the bitterness shouldn't dominate. It is also sweetened slightly by cooking. Here, the radicchio is simply grilled – it works really well with mozzarella but it's also good folded through roasted potato wedges.

Serves 4

4 heads of radicchio (such as di Treviso)
2 tablespoons olive oil
1 garlic clove, crushed
1 tablespoon chopped marjoram, plus more leaves to serve
1 tablespoon balsamic vinegar
2 teaspoons soft brown sugar
sea salt and freshly ground black pepper
250g good-quality mozzarella (sliced if a large ball)

Cut the radicchio into wedges lengthways, keeping the base intact so that the leaves stay attached.

Mix together the rest of the ingredients except the mozzarella, and place in a wide bowl. Heat a griddle pan or barbecue until very hot. Wilt the radicchio by grilling it quickly on the griddle plate, for about 30 seconds each side. (This may have to be done in batches.) As each batch comes from the griddle, mix whilst still hot in the dressing. Season well.

Serve the griddled radicchio with the mozzarella and sprinkle with marjoram leaves.

Mackerel Escabeche

Escabeche means pickled and you can use this method for any oily fish. The fish is fried, then pickled in spiced vinegar – it's important to add a bit of sugar at this point to balance the dish. It is very good just served on grilled sourdough with an autumn salad.

Serves 4–6

1 tablespoon fine cornmeal or polenta
1 teaspoon smoked paprika
1 tablespoon rice flour
sea salt and freshly ground black pepper
6 mackerel fillets
50ml olive oil

For the pickling mixture:
1 red onion, thinly sliced
2 garlic cloves, thinly sliced
1 red chilli, deseeded if preferred, thinly sliced
1 teaspoon ground fennel seeds
½ fennel bulb, thinly sliced
½ carrot, peeled and cut into batons
50ml good-quality red wine vinegar
1 bay leaf
1 tablespoon brown sugar
1 sprig of thyme
50ml olive oil

Place all the ingredients for the pickling mixture except the oil in a pan. Simmer for 10 minutes until well combined and the vegetables are tender. Remove from the heat. Add the oil and pour into a serving dish.

Mix the cornmeal, paprika and rice flour together. Season the mackerel fillets, then dust with the spiced mixture.

In a shallow pan, fry the fish in the hot oil until golden (about 2 minutes each side). Remove from the pan, drain and add to the pickling mixture immediately, making sure the fish is well covered. Leave at room temperature for about 1 hour for the flavours to develop.

Squash Gnudi

This is the best vegetarian dish by Ben Bulger, who works in the Field Kitchen with me. The gnudi are very like gnocchi. You can serve them as soon as they're ready – fry a couple of sage leaves with butter and add to the gnudi, along with some Parmesan. You can also leave them to go cold – either reheat in the oven, or fry in a non-stick pan with a little oil or butter.

Serves 4

400g squash, peeled, deseeded and chopped
1–2 tablespoons olive oil
250g ricotta cheese
150g Parmesan cheese, finely grated, plus more to serve
1 egg
pinch of grated nutmeg
sea salt and freshly ground black pepper
about 100g pasta flour

Sauté the squash in the oil until soft, then mash with a fork to a purée and leave to cool.

Add the cheeses, egg, nutmeg, salt and pepper.

Sift in the flour to form a dough (you may need to add a little more flour, depending on the wetness of the squash).

Roll into walnut-sized pieces and plop into a big pan of boiling water. They are done when they float to the top.

Drain and serve with more Parmesan and some sage butter.

Pan-fried Chicken Livers with Sage and Radicchio

Chicken livers are very quick to cook but it is absolutely essential that you don't leave them to cook for too long or they'll be ruined. They combine perfectly with bacon, sage and balsamic vinegar, and the radicchio gives a fresh contrast. You could, alternatively, serve the chicken livers with a winter salad and some cooked Puy lentils.

Serves 4

2 tablespoons olive oil
100g smoked streaky bacon or pancetta, cut into lardons
20 sage leaves
2 heads radicchio (ideally radicchio di Treviso)
1 teaspoon caster sugar
100ml plus 1 teaspoon balsamic vinegar
sea salt and freshly ground black pepper
500g chicken livers, trimmed
1 tablespoon crème fraîche

Heat half the oil in a non-stick pan and cook the bacon lardons until slightly browned, then remove with a slotted spoon. Add the sage leaves to the pan and cook until crisp, stirring all the time; remove and add to the bacon.

Cut the Treviso into thin wedges lengthways and wilt it for a few seconds each side on a hot griddle pan, moving it quickly so as not to burn. Toss in the remaining oil, sugar and the 1 teaspoon balsamic vinegar and season well. Mix in half the sage and bacon. Keep warm.

Heat the bacon pan until very hot and add the chicken livers. Brown all over to seal, shaking the pan so they don't catch. Reduce the heat and cook for about 4 minutes.

Add the remaining 100ml balsamic vinegar, increase the heat and reduce the liquid for a minute. Finish with the crème fraîche and fold through.

Arrange the warm Treviso salad on a warmed serving dish. Top with the chicken livers, drizzle over the sauce and sprinkle with the rest of the bacon and sage.

Spiced Turnip, Potato and Squash Gratin

This is a slightly unusual type of gratin based on one by the Australian chef Christine Manfield. The recipe below is only a guide – the gratin is very open to variation. You could make it with a number of other root vegetables, for example parsnips, celeriac or Jerusalem artichokes. Add extra chilli if you'd like it hotter.

Serves 6

400g squash
2 large turnips
500g potatoes
2 garlic cloves, crushed
1 egg yolk
150ml plain yoghurt
sea salt and freshly ground plain black pepper
2 teaspoons harissa paste

Preheat the oven to 180°C/Gas Mark 4.

Peel all the vegetables and cut them into 5mm-thick slices.

Mix the rest of the ingredients together to make a spice paste.

In a large gratin dish, place alternate layers of the vegetables, brushing each piece with the spice paste as you layer.

Cover and bake in the oven for about 1 hour, or until tender.

SUNDAY

Pot-roasted Guineafowl with Coppa, Sage and Rosemary

The gravy in this dish is full of rich flavour. Make sure you don't overcook the guineafowl breasts, but equally be sure the legs are cooked through. Cooking them separately will help with this, but check carefully. You can use the wings, giblets and backbone of the guineafowl to make stock.

Serves 6

2 guineafowl
8–10 slices coppa di Parma, or prosciutto
1 tablespoon olive oil
15g unsalted butter
sea salt and freshly ground black pepper
6 sprigs of rosemary
leaves from 1 bunch of sage
6 garlic cloves, peeled
150ml dark rum
150ml dry sherry
300ml chicken stock
150ml double cream

Pull the legs away from the body of the guineafowl, cut through the skin and twist each leg to remove the ball from the socket joint. Cut through the joint to remove the legs completely. Cut the wings from the carcass. Holding the crown of the carcass upright, cut down each side of the backbone to remove the breasts. Wrap the breasts with ham and tie with kitchen string.

Heat the oil and butter in a large pan. Brown the legs and breasts well on all sides and season with salt and pepper. Add the herbs and garlic and, before the garlic browns, add the booze and stock. Cook for about 40 minutes, turning the legs and breasts frequently, over a medium heat.

When the breasts are almost done (they will be firm to the touch), remove from the pan and leave to rest. Increase the heat, when the juices are syrupy, add the cream and season. Slice the breasts. Cut the legs into two. Pour over the juices and serve.

Warm Salad of Grilled Leeks, Fennel and Roasted Romanesco

Depending on the time of year, you could add cauliflower or purple sprouting broccoli to this versatile warm salad. To get the best results, keep the salad dressing just warm and add each vegetable as soon as it's cooked.

Serves 4–6

3 leeks
1 fennel bulb
1 head romanesco, separated into florets
2 tablespoons olive oil

For the dressing:
juice of 1 lemon
2 teaspoons caster sugar
1 tablespoon white wine
1 tablespoon good-quality white wine vinegar
1 garlic clove, crushed
pinch of fennel seeds, crushed
pinch of ground allspice
3 tablespoons extra virgin olive oil, plus more to drizzle
sea salt and freshly ground black pepper
1 teaspoon chopped tarragon

Preheat the oven to 180°C/Gas Mark 4. Heat all the dressing ingredients except the tarragon together in a large pan and leave to cool and infuse.

Wash the leeks and blanch them in boiling water for 5 minutes, drain, then split them in half lengthways. Trim the fennel and cut into very thin slices. Grill the leeks on a griddle pan until slightly charred, then cut into 2.5–5cm pieces. Grill the fennel until wilted and add to the dressing with the leeks.

Toss the romanesco in the olive oil, season and roast in the oven for 15–20 minutes, until just cooked through and slightly brown. Add to the dressing.

Toss the vegetables together, season well, drizzle with the extra virgin olive oil and sprinkle with the tarragon.

Swiss Chard, Squash and Blue Cheese Torte

This is one of our most popular vegetarian main courses in the Field Kitchen that meat-eaters are guaranteed to want to eat too. The squash, blue cheese and pecans are a good combination – we sometimes use them just to scatter over autumn salad from our polytunnels.

Serves 6–8

75g pecan nuts
pinch of cayenne pepper
dash of Tabasco sauce
½ teaspoon sea salt
1 butternut squash (or other variety if preferred)
2 tablespoons olive oil, plus more for drizzling
sea salt and freshly ground black pepper
2 garlic cloves, finely chopped
2 small onions, sliced
300g Swiss chard or spinach
200g blue cheese, chopped (we use Devon Blue)
1 blind-baked shortcrust pastry case (see page 244)
50g Parmesan cheese, finely grated
20 sage leaves
15g unsalted butter

Preheat the oven to 200°C/Gas Mark 6.

Mix together the pecans, cayenne, Tabasco and salt and place on a baking tray. Bake in the oven for 5–6 minutes until lightly toasted.

Peel the squash, cut in half and remove the seeds, then cut into rough 2cm cubes. Place on a baking tray, drizzle with olive oil, season and bake for about 30 minutes in the oven, until the squash is tender.

Sprinkle with the garlic and return to the oven for a further 5 minutes, then allow to cool.

Cook the onions gently in the 2 tablespoons of olive oil for about 20 minutes, until soft but not brown. Meanwhile, separate the chard stalks from the leaves. Chop the stalks roughly and blanch in boiling salted water for 4 minutes.

Remove with a slotted spoon and set aside. Blanch the chard leaves for 1 minute, drain, then refresh under cold running water. Squeeze any excess water out of the chard and add both the stalks and leaves to the onions. Mix until thoroughly combined and season well.

In a large bowl, gently combine the pecans, squash, chard and blue cheese. Tip into the pastry case and sprinkle with the Parmesan. Return to the oven for about 10 minutes.

Cook the sage leaves in the butter until crisp, and use to garnish the finished torte.

Plum, Blackberry (or Blueberry) and Amaretti Crumble

A perfect autumn pudding. Blackberries or blueberries are a great addition to a simple plum crumble – giving a bit of extra flavour and deepening the colour. In the Field Kitchen at this time of year we can use blueberries grown on Dartmoor. The amaretti topping can also be used on apple and pear crumbles.

Serves 8–10

2kg plums, quartered and stoned
300g blueberries or blackberries
4 tablespoons soft brown sugar
finely grated zest and juice of 2 oranges
slug of booze – brandy, rum or Amaretto

For the crumble:
350g plain flour
250g unsalted butter
200g caster sugar
100g oats
100g crushed amaretti biscuits

Preheat the oven to 150°C/Gas Mark 2.

Mix the fruit with the other ingredients and tip into a 2-litre shallow pudding dish.

Put the flour into a food processor and add the butter, in knobs. Process until the mixture is just past the 'breadcrumb' stage. Remove, place in a bowl and add the rest of the crumble ingredients. Rub and mix in further with your fingertips so the crumble is lumpy and not dry.

Top the fruit with the crumble topping and bake for 45 minutes.

Everyday

Stir-fried Swede
Callaloo Soup
Aromatic Pumpkin
Anna's Moroccan Beetroot Salad
Squash Hummus
Spiced Veggie Cakes
Lamb, Barley and Root Vegetable Broth
Pumpkin Muffins
Anna's Red Wine Risotto with Radicchio and Gorgonzola
Simple Squash Soup from Manna from Devon
Radicchio Pasta
Thai Pumpkin Soup

Sunday

Sweet Potato and Rosemary Gratin
Venison Pie
Braised Red Russian Kale
Brown Sugar Meringues with Pears, Pecans and Chocolate

NOVEMBER

Into the gloom

November can be a dismal month in Devon: farmers call it 'the long back end' because, bathed in warm, damp air off the Atlantic, grass and cereals continue growing long after they have become dormant further east. Even the cows lose their appetite for the dank, watery growth that results from a warm and active soil, releasing more nitrogen than there is sunlight to build into good leaves. For the good of my vegetables and my mood I long for the hard frosts of winter proper that tend to arrive towards Christmas.

Pappy veg

It can be a poor month for vegetables, with plenty available but very little at its best. It is possible still to be harvesting lettuce, broccoli, even tomatoes and strawberries under tunnels or glass but the flavour is dreadful; better not to cling to the coat-tails of summer but to move on to proper winter roots and greens. Parsnips, Savoy and kale all taste better once they have had some proper cold on them, so we look forward to some frost to stop the pappy growth and stiffen up our winter veg. Swedes, though not yet at their best, can be good and start making a regular appearance in the veg boxes. Cavolo nero and red Russian kale, which I first saw growing as an ornamental on a roundabout in Spain, are often both good, but curly kale is definitely best left until it has had some hard frost.

Bitter leaves

One exception to this doom and gloom is the radicchio, escarole and endive family, which seems to thrive in the late autumn. These dandelion relatives look like lettuce but their true origin is given away by an intense earthy bitterness, which I love: an antidote to November's dreary blandness. Small amounts can be used in salads, balanced by a sweet dressing or the addition of fruit (such as mango, dried cranberries or even cubes of roasted squash) but radicchio, in particular, is more commonly cooked in its native Italy. One of my favourite recipes at this time of year is radicchio risotto, closely followed by a radicchio pasta. Both are good on their own but possibly even better for the addition of some smoked streaky bacon (Jane might say prosciutto). I suspect that in our dim light the local crop has even more bitterness than imports from further south, so consider reducing the quantities recommended in Italian recipes to avoid overwhelming a dish.

Fractal brassicas

Romanescos represent the best of the novelty vegetables. I have no time for yellow courgettes and am dubious of the virtues of variegated beetroot, but these pointed green cauliflower relatives with their extraordinary self-repeating, fractal curds not only excite the mathematical nerds and the restless searchers for novelty, they also taste great. Romanescos originate from Italy. Not surprisingly, they are susceptible to hard frost but they retain their quality in lower light and thrive in the damp gloom of a Devon November. They keep their colour and some crunch when cooked (within reason) and have a nutty flavour. Anything you can do with a cauliflower is better with romanesco. They can also be good substitutes for broccoli, making it seem bland and insipid by comparison. Jane's favoured method is to roast them for 15 minutes and serve them with a stiff dressing.

Celeriac harvest

Towards the end of the month we start harvesting celeriac with the aim of having it in store before the first hard frosts. This smoky, celery-flavoured root will keep in the fridge for months if healthy at harvest and not frost-damaged. We often store it through to March, and the Dutch, with their dark mastery of storage, manage to keep it through to May. It lends its flavour well to stocks, a mash (mixed with potatoes), or grated into the classic celeriac remoulade, but my favourite is celeriac soup, with a little truffle oil if I'm feeling extravagant.

Quick and easy ideas
ROMANESCO

Whole

Coat a whole romanesco in olive oil and roast in a medium oven for 15 minutes or until tender. Make a dressing with the zest and juice of 1 lemon, some olive oil, a pinch of cayenne, some chopped, peeled red pepper and crushed garlic. Break up the romanesco, pour the dressing over and mix well. Leave at room temperature for 30 minutes, then serve.

Deep-fried romanesco

Dip raw romanesco in Bhaji Batter (page 86) and cook in hot oil for 5–7 minutes. Serve with Beetroot Tzatziki (page 173).

A very easy pasta dish

Cook sliced garlic and dried chilli in some olive oil. Add cooked (blanched) romanesco florets and cook briefly, mixing well. Season. Toss with cooked ditalini (little tubes) or penne pasta and some of the pasta cooking water. Take off the heat and fold through some grated pecorino.

Quick romanesco cheese

Try tossing just-cooked romanesco with crumbled Stilton, crème fraiche and chives.

Cauliflower or romanesco

Use in any recipe instead of cauliflower.

EVERYDAY

Stir-fried Swede

I always eat swede mashed, with onion or carrot, but I decided to ask around for any other inspiring recipes. Darran, who does the farm tours at Riverford, received this one from a friend who knew a Thai lady living in Orkney, like you do!

Serves 4–6

1 swede
2 garlic cloves, crushed
2cm piece fresh root ginger, grated
25g unsalted butter
1 tablespoon sesame oil
1 tablespoon soy sauce
juice of 1 lemon
1 tablespoon toasted sesame seeds
1 tablespoon chopped coriander

Peel the swede and cut into matchsticks as thinly as possible. Cook the garlic and ginger in the butter and sesame oil for 2 minutes, add the swede and mix well. Add 100ml water, increase the heat, cover and cook for 10 minutes. Uncover, add the soy sauce and lemon juice and cook for another 5 minutes, stirring, until the swede is cooked and the sauce reduced.

Sprinkle with sesame seeds and coriander.

Callaloo Soup

Famous in the Caribbean, this soup is made there with leaves from dasheen or taro bush. The original soup has a very green, earthy flavour, which I think the kale works well to recreate, but you could also try making it with spinach or chard.

Serves 4–6

1 onion, finely chopped
1 celery stick, chopped
½ leek, chopped
100g smoked streaky bacon, cut into small strips
1 tablespoon sunflower oil
3 garlic cloves, crushed
¼ teaspoon thyme leaves
1 chilli, deseeded if preferred, finely chopped
400g kale leaves, tough stalks removed, chopped
pinch of ground cloves
800ml hot chicken stock, plus more if needed
200ml tinned coconut milk
200g picked white crab meat
sea salt and freshly ground black pepper
hot pepper sauce, to taste

In a large pan, cook the onion, celery, leek and bacon in the sunflower oil for about 10 minutes, until soft but not brown. To this, add the garlic, thyme, chilli, kale, cloves and stock and simmer for 10 minutes. Add the coconut milk. Bring to a simmer and blend in a liquidiser, adding more stock if required.

Return to the pan and add the crab meat.

Season well, adding hot pepper sauce to taste.

November

Aromatic Pumpkin

Generally, in the Field Kitchen, we like to roast squash and pumpkin, but here it is braised in a sweetened, aromatic water. It's a great technique, as it allows the squash flesh to be infused with the flavour of the spices. Serve the pumpkin and the aromatic cooking water with plain couscous.

Serves 4–6

finely grated zest and juice of 1 orange
1 onion, finely chopped
pinch of freshly ground black pepper
½ teaspoon ground ginger
½ teaspoon ground cinnamon
½ teaspoon sea salt
25g unsalted butter
pinch of saffron
1kg pumpkin or squash, cut into 3cm chunks (prepared weight)
1 tablespoon icing sugar
few drops of orange blossom water
handful of mint or coriander leaves, chopped

Place all the ingredients up to the pumpkin in a pan and pour in 400ml water. Simmer together for 10 minutes.

Add the pumpkin and cook slowly for about 15 minutes until tender. Add the icing sugar and orange blossom water, and cook for a couple more minutes.

Sprinkle with the herbs.

Anna's Moroccan Beetroot Salad

Riverford Cook Anna Colquhoun often uses flavours from North African and Mediterranean cuisine, inspired by her culinary travels. This is a good way to spice up stored beetroot as winter approaches.

Serves 4

600g beetroot, washed
3 tablespoons olive oil
2 tablespoons red wine vinegar
finely grated zest of 1 orange and juice of 2
½ teaspoon icing sugar
½ teaspoon cinnamon
pinch of cayenne pepper
3 tablespoons chopped mint
sea salt and freshly ground black pepper
2 tablespoons plain yoghurt

Preheat the oven to 190°C/Gas Mark 5.

Toss the beetroot in a little of the olive oil and place on a baking tray where they will fit snugly. Add 200ml water, cover with foil and place in the hot oven for about 1 hour, or until tender. When cool enough to handle, remove the skin from the beetroot and trim. Cut into bite-size pieces.

Whisk together the rest of the ingredients except the yoghurt. Pour over the warm beetroot, mix well and check the seasoning.

Leave for at least an hour at room temperature before serving, drizzled with seasoned yoghurt.

Squash Hummus

A recipe from Mark Bader, one of our Riverford Cooks working around Brighton. It's a different take on basic, plain hummus and the roasted squash makes the end result wonderfully sweet. Serve simply with toasted flatbread or pitta bread.

Makes 500–700ml/Serves 10

1 butternut squash, deseeded and chopped
juice of 1 lemon, plus more to taste
1 large garlic clove
2 tablespoons tahini
sea salt and freshly ground black pepper
handful of toasted pine nuts
olive oil, to drizzle

Preheat the oven to 200°C/Gas Mark 6.

Roast the squash in the oven for 30 minutes, or until very tender and soft. Scrape the flesh from the skin into a food processor, add the lemon juice (you may need extra depending on taste), garlic, tahini, salt and pepper and blitz until smooth. Check the seasoning.

Place in a small bowl with the toasted pine nuts scattered over and drizzled with the olive oil.

Spiced Veggie Cakes

It's important, for this recipe, to cook the potatoes in their skins. If you don't, they'll absorb water and the mixture will be too wet. It's also a recipe for which it's worth investing in some gram (chickpea) flour, as this binds together slightly wet vegetable mixtures very well. Serve with a dollop of Beetroot Tzatziki (see page 173).

Serves 6–8

2 potatoes (about 350g)
sea salt and freshly ground black pepper
400g butternut squash, peeled and cut into 1cm pieces
200g canned chickpeas, drained
1 tablespoon ground cumin
1 tablespoon ground coriander
4 tablespoons vegetable oil
1 tablespoon brown mustard seeds
2 tablespoons finely chopped coriander leaves
100–150g plain flour or gram flour, to dust

Preheat the oven to 200°C/Gas Mark 6.

Place the potatoes in a saucepan of cold salted water. Bring to the boil over a high heat and boil for 15 minutes, or until tender. Drain, cool slightly, then peel and cut into 1cm pieces.

Roast the squash in the hot oven for 20 minutes, then add it to the potato. Add the chickpeas, cumin and coriander and mix to just combine.

Heat 1 tablespoon of the vegetable oil in a large frying pan over a high heat, add the mustard seeds and cook until they begin to pop. Add them to the vegetable mixture with the coriander leaves, season to taste and gently mix until combined. Using wet hands, form the mixture into small patties and refrigerate for 30 minutes.

Heat the remaining oil in a large frying pan over a high heat. Dust the patties in flour, add to the frying pan and cook, in batches, for 2 minutes each side, or until golden.

Lamb, Barley and Root Vegetable Broth

This is essentially a Scotch broth. It takes a little time to make, but only so that the meat cooks long enough to become tender; the actual preparation isn't too time-consuming. I really like to cook with pearl barley – having been underused for a time, it seems to be coming back into fashion. You can use it in broths such as this one, but also in salads (in place of farro, see page 216) or as a nutty alternative to rice in risotto.

Serves 6

500g lamb shoulder, cut into 2cm chunks
2 tablespoons olive oil
25g unsalted butter
1 onion, finely chopped
1 celery stick, finely chopped
1 leek, finely chopped
1 sprig of thyme
1.5 litres chicken stock
100g pearl barley
600g mixed root vegetables – carrots, turnips, swedes and celeriac, finely
   chopped
sea salt and freshly ground black pepper
1 tablespoon chopped parsley

Brown the lamb shoulder in the very hot oil in a large, heavy-based pan. Remove with a slotted spoon and add the butter, onion, celery, leek and thyme. Cook slowly for 10 minutes before returning the lamb to the pan along with the stock.

Bring to a simmer and cook for 30 minutes. Add the barley and cook for 30 minutes more. Add the root vegetables and simmer for 30 minutes until lamb, barley and veg are all tender.

Season and sprinkle with chopped parsley.

Pumpkin Muffins

Using pumpkin in muffins and scones is a very Antipodean thing to do. We tried these out for Halloween and were quite surprised at how good they were. They would be fun to make with children. To cook the squash, I think it's best to peel and chop it up, then sweat it very gently in some unsalted butter (half cover so that it steams a little) until soft.

Makes 14

115g unsalted butter
175g dark brown muscovado sugar
115g golden syrup or honey
1 egg, beaten
225g cooked and mashed pumpkin or squash
200g self-raising flour
pinch of sea salt
1½ teaspoons ground cinnamon
1 teaspoon grated nutmeg
75g currants or raisins

Preheat the oven to 200°C/Gas Mark 6. Place 12 muffin cases in a muffin tray.

In a large bowl, cream the butter until soft. Add the sugar and syrup or honey and beat until light and fluffy.

Stir in the egg and pumpkin until well mixed. Sift over the flour, salt, cinnamon and nutmeg. Lightly fold these ingredients into the mixture.

Stir in the currants or raisins. Spoon the mixture into the muffin cases so each is two-thirds full. Bake in the centre of the oven for 12–15 minutes, until a skewer inserted in the centre comes out clean.

Anna's Red Wine Risotto with Radicchio and Gorgonzola

Another wonderful recipe from Riverford Cook Anna Colquhoun – a rich risotto, but cut through with the fresher taste of radicchio. It's important to use a decent red wine, as it's such a significant part of the final flavour.

Serves 4

1 onion, finely chopped
2 celery sticks, finely chopped
1 leek, finely chopped
1 tablespoon olive oil
50g unsalted butter
2 garlic cloves, crushed
5 sage leaves, finely chopped
300g arborio rice
sea salt and freshly ground black pepper
500ml good Italian dry red wine
600–900ml hot chicken stock
1 head radicchio, halved, cored and thinly sliced
2 tablespoons finely grated Parmesan cheese
75g toasted walnuts, roughly chopped
100g Gorgonzola cheese, chopped

Cook the onion, celery and leek slowly in a large pan in the olive oil and half the butter for about 10 minutes. Add the garlic, sage and rice, increase the heat and stir vigorously for 2 minutes. Season well. Add half the wine and bring to a gentle simmer, stirring slowly all the time. When it is almost absorbed, add the rest of the wine and simmer gently until it too is almost absorbed. Now start to add the hot chicken stock, a ladle at a time, only adding more stock when the rest has been absorbed. Continue for about 10 minutes. Add the radicchio and continue to cook, adding stock as required, for another 5 minutes.

Now the rice should be almost cooked but still with some bite to it. Add the Parmesan and half the walnuts and allow to cook for 2 more minutes, adding a little extra stock if required so the risotto has a sloppy consistency.

Remove from the heat, add the Gorgonzola and the remaining butter. Fold through gently, and check the seasoning. Serve topped with rest of the walnuts.

Simple Squash Soup from Manna from Devon

This was a soup that Holly Jones, from Manna from Devon, cooked as part of a demo we did at Dartmouth Food Festival. Holly runs a cookery school with her husband, David, in Kingswear and they are a major driving force behind the festival. I particularly like this soup finished with chilli and horseradish.

Serves 4

1 leek, finely chopped
1 squash, peeled and chopped
1 tablespoon olive oil
1 garlic clove, crushed
sea salt and freshly ground black pepper
enough chicken or vegetable stock to cover (about 1 litre)
2 teaspoons South Devon Chilli Farm jam
1 teaspoon grated horseradish

Cook the leek and squash in the olive oil until softening, then add the garlic and stir for 1 minute. Season well, cover with chicken stock and simmer for about 20 minutes, until tender. Blend until smooth. Check the seasoning.

Serve in bowls with a blob of chilli jam and some grated horseradish.

Radicchio Pasta

This cream-based sauce is based on a pasta dish I learnt at the River Café and it's one of Guy's favourites. It's a quick and simple way of making under-appreciated radicchio into a great-tasting dish.

Serves 4

1 large onion, finely sliced
1 tablespoon olive oil, plus more if needed
25g unsalted butter
250g smoked streaky bacon, rind removed, or prosciutto, chopped into
    long strips
a few sage leaves, torn (optional)
150g radicchio, shredded
400g linguine, fettuccine or, ideally, pappardelle if you can get it
50ml double cream, plus more if needed
juice of 1 lemon
sea salt and freshly ground black pepper
50g Parmesan cheese, grated, plus more if needed

Fry the onion in the oil and butter in a heavy-based saucepan until translucent.

Add the bacon or ham and fry until starting to colour, then toss in the sage (if using). Add the radicchio, stir and cook until collapsed, adding a little more oil if necessary. Meanwhile, cook the pasta according to the packet directions. When the pasta is almost done, add the cream and lemon juice to the sauce. Season, add the Parmesan and taste; if you find it a little too bitter, add more cream and Parmesan. Toss the sauce with the drained pasta.

Thai Pumpkin Soup

We hold an annual pumpkin day in Devon and at Riverford's other farms around the country: this soup is a great success with visitors. When preparing the pumpkin it is silly to waste the hairy insides and seeds – they make a great stock to use in this soup (with a more 'pumpkiny' flavour) or in other versions of squash soup or risottos.

Serves 4

1kg pumpkin, deseeded, peeled and chopped (reserve the trimmings)
1 onion, finely chopped, plus ½ onion
2 celery sticks, finely chopped
2 carrots, peeled and finely chopped
1 leek top, washed and chopped
2 tablespoons sunflower oil
2 tablespoons Thai red curry paste
sea salt and freshly ground black pepper
400ml tin coconut milk
large handful of coriander leaves
1 tablespoon brown sugar
1 tablespoon lemon juice
fish sauce, to taste

First make a pumpkin stock. Put all the pumpkin insides and seeds in a large pan, add the ½ onion, 1 each of the celery sticks and carrots and the leek top. Cover with water and simmer for 30 minutes. Strain.

Warm the oil in a soup pot, add the curry paste and cook for 5 minutes, stirring continuously. Add the vegetables and season, reduce the heat and cook for 15 minutes, stirring to stop any browning. Add 1 litre of the pumpkin stock, bring to a boil and simmer for about 5 minutes, or until the pumpkin is tender. Purée in a blender (if you want to be a perfectionist you could also sieve it at this point). Return to a boil and whisk in the coconut milk. Add the coriander leaves and finish with the brown sugar, lemon juice and a dash of fish sauce to taste.

SUNDAY

Sweet Potato and Rosemary Gratin

This was first cooked for me by Mr Sam Clark (from Moro restaurant in London) many, many years ago, on my birthday. It is one of those wonderful dishes that once tasted is never forgotten. We always make this in the Field Kitchen when we get the first sweet potatoes from our growers in southern Spain at this time of year.

Serves 6–8

500g sweet potatoes, peeled and thinly sliced on a mandolin or carefully by hand
500g potatoes, peeled and thinly sliced on a mandolin or carefully by hand
sea salt and freshly ground black pepper
200ml double cream
50ml milk
1 chilli, deseeded if preferred, finely chopped
leaves from 1 sprig of rosemary, chopped
2 garlic cloves, crushed
1 tablespoon finely grated Parmesan cheese

Preheat the oven to 180°C/Gas Mark 4.

Layer the potato and sweet potato alternately in a gratin dish, seasoning as you go.

Bring the cream and milk to a boil, add the chilli, rosemary and garlic and pour over the potatoes; it should fill half the dish. Finish with the Parmesan.

Cover with foil and bake in the oven for at least 1 hour, or until tender, uncovering for the final 30 minutes.

Venison Pie

Venison is best from November through to March, and goes perfectly with the vegetables that are available at this time of year (it is available through the Riverford meat boxes too, for a short season between September and November from a couple of well-established herds in the West Country). Marinating the venison before cooking, then using the marinade as part of the sauce, is the key to what makes this dish taste so good. Using suet in the crust is also quite special, and a little naughty, but it does make particularly good pastry (try using it in Yorkshire pudding too). You could use a normal shortcrust pastry if you prefer.

Serves 6–8

For the marinade:
1 onion, finely chopped
1 celery stick, finely chopped
1 carrot, finely chopped
5 garlic cloves, chopped
375ml red wine
2 tablespoons red wine vinegar
1 teaspoon sea salt
1 teaspoon thyme leaves
2 bay leaves
3 juniper berries
6 black peppercorns

For the filling:
1.25kg venison shoulder, cut into 3cm chunks
2 tablespoons plain flour, seasoned
1 tablespoon olive oil
15g unsalted butter
3 onions, finely chopped
100g smoked streaky bacon, cut into lardons
1 teaspoon freshly ground black pepper
grated nutmeg
½ teaspoon ground allspice
1 teaspoon ground coriander
200ml beef stock
150g prunes, chopped

finely grated zest and juice of 1 orange
125g peeled, vacuum-packed chestnuts, roughly chopped (optional)

For the suet crust:
350g self-raising flour, plus more to dust
175g beef suet
sea salt and freshly ground black pepper

Mix together the marinade ingredients. Mix with the venison, cover and marinate for 24–48 hours in the fridge. Remove the venison from the marinade and strain and reserve the marinade. Dry the meat on kitchen paper and toss in the seasoned flour. Brown in the hot oil and butter in a large pan, in batches if necessary.

Remove the meat from the pan, add the onions and bacon and cook for 10 minutes, until the onions are soft. Add the spices and cook for 1 more minute before adding the reserved marinade and beef stock. Return the venison and bring to a boil, scraping the bottom of the pan and mixing well. Add the prunes and orange zest and juice and simmer over a very low heat for 1½–2 hours, until the meat is tender. At this point, add the chestnuts (if using), check the seasoning and cool.

While the venison is cooling, make the pastry. Mix the flour, suet, salt and pepper together and add enough cold water to make a soft dough. Preheat the oven to 220°C/Gas Mark 7.

Transfer the cold meat mixture to a pie dish (approx. 20cm x 20cm).

Roll out the pastry and cut a 2cm strip that will sit on the rim of the pie dish. Dampen the dish and press the strip all around the rim. Roll out the pastry on a floured work surface, wet the pastry rim and top with the pastry lid. Press around the edges and do some fancy fluting or crimping if you like. Make a small hole in the centre and bake in the hot oven for 30 minutes.

Braised Red Russian Kale

This is a really quick way of cooking kale, and it works best with the softer varieties, such as red Russian kale. You could stir through a few tablespoons of cooked Puy lentils or white beans at the end of cooking to make this a simple, vegetarian main course, otherwise it can be served as a side dish with the venison pie.

Serves 4–6

1 tablespoon olive oil
1 onion, finely chopped
1 teaspoon sea salt
freshly ground black pepper
1 dried chilli, stalk removed, deseeded if preferred, chopped (optional)
4 garlic cloves, crushed
400g red Russian kale, washed, tough stalks removed
500ml hot chicken or vegetable stock
juice of ½ lemon
drizzle of good-quality olive oil

Heat the olive oil in a pan, add the onion, salt, pepper and chilli (if using), and cook for 3 minutes. Add the garlic, stir, and quickly follow with the kale and stock. Cook for 5–8 minutes, stirring occasionally. Finish with the lemon juice and good oil, and check the seasoning.

Brown Sugar Meringues with Pears, Pecans and Chocolate

This dessert deserves to be dressed up as much as possible. Sometimes we add custard or caramel sauce along with all the other toppings – the messier and more flamboyant it is, the better. In the summer, we serve the meringues with poached rhubarb and custard.

Serves 6

For the meringues:
4 egg whites
100g caster sugar
100g dark muscovado sugar
drop of vanilla extract

For the pears:
4 pears
250g caster sugar

For the rest:
400ml double cream
2 tablespoons toasted pecans, chopped
2 tablespoons maple syrup, plus more to taste
1 teaspoon brandy
100g dark chocolate

Preheat the oven to 110°C/Gas Mark ¼.

Beat the egg whites until they are just holding their shape, then gradually add the sugars a tablespoon at a time, beating continuously until all the sugar has been added and the mixture is stiff and glossy. Beat in the vanilla.

Spoon on to a baking tray lined with baking parchment in 6 blobs and, using a spoon, flatten each slightly. Bake for about 2 hours in the very low oven (each oven behaves differently, so it is important to keep an eye on them), until crisp on the outside and they come away easily from the baking parchment.

Peel the pears and cut into quarters. Cut each quarter into 3 wedges. Place in a pan with the sugar and 250ml water and poach gently for 15 minutes. Allow to cool.

Whip the double cream to soft peaks, then beat in the nuts, syrup and booze.

Melt the chocolate in a double boiler or in a bowl over a pan of simmering water (making sure the base of the bowl does not touch the water) until runny.

Place a spoonful of cream on each meringue, top with some pears and drizzle with the chocolate. Add extra maple syrup to taste.

Everyday

Sprout, Swede and Potato Hash
Sweet and Sour Red Cabbage
Windy City Salad
Leek and Blue Cheese Sauce
Chestnut and Squash Soup with Bacon and Sage
Potato Pizza
Baked Sprouts with a Stuffing Crust
Roast Parsnips with a Yoghurt and Date Sauce
Potato, Jerusalem Artichoke and Porcini Gratin
Stuffed Dates with Clementines and Pomegranates

Sunday

Partridge and Cabbage
Celeriac and Chestnut Pie
Cumberland Sauce
Mixed Winter Vegetables with Brown Butter and Almonds
Sticky Toffee Pudding

DECEMBER

Time for a rest

The extraordinary quantity of vegetables consumed at Christmas only goes to emphasise how little veg is consumed the rest of the year. Whatever your religious disposition, the mid-winter feast is a chance to celebrate the best of our culinary traditions and for once that includes large quantities of fresh vegetables. It is a hectic time for us, when we have to make use of every hour of the limited daylight and pray that frost does not interrupt the harvest. Not to deliver good sprouts in Christmas week is an unforgivable failure. One particularly desperate year we even had a team of people removing aphids from them with scrubbing brushes.

Flavourful feasting

Roots are at their best, whether freshly dug, such as parsnips, swede and root artichokes, or from the store, such as potatoes and carrots. We find the carrots taste better if dug in the autumn and barn-stored. The hardy greens like Savoy and kale also come into their own, and are at their best after being exposed to some frost. Red cabbage, another staple of Christmas, whether braised with apple or with beetroot and orange, can normally stand in the field to Christmas in Devon, but will succumb to really hard weather, so is more commonly harvested and cold-stored through the winter.

Sprout stalks and crosses

Of all the edible brassica family members (such as cabbage, cauliflower, swede and broccoli), Brussels sprouts have retained most of the bitter flavour inherited from their wild, kale-like ancestors, still found growing on the maritime fringes of western Europe. For one course of one meal a year, the nation suspends its quest for sweetness and celebrates this extraordinary vegetable. Borne on a tough trunk, supporting a canopy of leaves above, are dozens of spiralling bitter buds, whose development has been arrested by the efforts of generations of plant breeders. Using different varieties, they can be in season from September to February, but are at their best around Christmas, once we have had some hard frosts. Plant breeders are progressively increasing sweetness and reducing bitterness in modern varieties, as well as selecting for buds that develop uniformly and synchronously up the stalk, allowing a single, mechanised harvest rather than the more traditional sequential picking from the bottom up.

With their canopy of upper leaves trapping humidity, sprouts are prone to a host of insect pests and fungal diseases, which are hard to control organically

without an armoury of pesticides, so we still pick selectively by hand. Sprout tops (the loose, tennis-ball-sized apical bud) were traditionally picked in November and December to remove apical dominance and encourage the development of juvenile sprouts higher up the stalk. They can sometimes provide good eating but can also be excessively tough and bitter, according to variety and maturity; worth a try if you are a gardener, but inspect for aphids and perhaps have a chew before parting with cash for them. We sometimes leave the sprouts on the stalk in the boxes – partly because they keep better and partly because they look so great.

Is it worth crossing the stalk of the sprout with a knife? I would normally say life is too short, but if the sample is varied in size I sometimes cut the larger ones to speed their cooking and avoid overdoing the smaller ones. If you tire of plain boiled sprouts, try Jane's Baked Sprouts with a Stuffing Crust (see page 335), or shred them and stir-fry with garlic, chilli and ginger or with bacon and some toasted almonds.

Some time, normally towards the end of the month, growth finally stops for the year. Even in southern California, where their December is like our June, growers tell me that there is a period of dormancy when very little happens in the fields. It will be six weeks before we see any significant new growth, and in that time some crops like leeks can actually shrink as they lose leaves to winter storms. At the point when growth stops we need to have enough crop standing ready to harvest in the field to see us through until growth starts again in late January. It all depends on having got planting dates right back in the summer, when we have to assume an 'average year'. However, as no two years are the same something usually goes wrong, often providing a glut in November and leaving us short at Christmas.

Champion cauliflower

The one exception to this dormancy is the winter cauliflower (known locally as broccoli, don't ask me why), which somehow 'grows from its stump', sacrificing outer leaves and shrinking back in stature while secretly making its delicate curd, protected from all but the hardest frost by a tight wrapping of inner leaves. Could cauliflower be the next beetroot, saved from the scrapheap of sulphurous mundanity by a championing celebrity chef? We hope so, because the maritime fringe of the south-west, along with the Isle of Thanet in Kent, once had a thriving industry supplying their creamy-white curds through the winter; so much so that the area east of Penzance was known as the Golden Mile on account of the fortunes made out of winter

cauliflower and early potatoes. Cauliflower is much prized in the Far East and southern Europe (where it is often too hot for them to grow well), and in northern Europe (where the winters are too cold) – just about everywhere except here in the UK where they grow so well twelve months of the year and yet are regarded as the lowest of the low. The mushy over-boiled cauliflower of school-dinner memories and the ubiquitous pre-cooked and reheated abomination from many a pub kitchen, have no doubt hastened the decline. Beetroot, rhubarb and gooseberries came back from the brink of extinction, so perhaps there is hope, if only we stop boiling it to death. Cauliflower cheese with a baked potato will always make a good weekday supper, but try roasting it and adding it to pasta with chilli and garlic, or in a soup, or deep-fried, tempura style.

Quick and easy ideas
BRUSSELS SPROUTS

Stir-fried sprouts

Shred sprouts and stir-fry with diced chorizo. Toss with toasted flaked almonds.

Roasted sprouts

Roast quartered sprouts in a medium oven with olive oil and salt and pepper. Sprinkle with toasted breadcrumbs, lemon zest and parsley.

Sprout and pine nut pasta

Cook finely chopped onion and shredded sprouts in olive oil until almost tender. Cook fusilli pasta until al dente. Drain and reserve about 100ml pasta cooking water. Add to the sprouts and cook for another few minutes until tender. In a separate pan, heat a knob of butter until it turns brown and gives off a nutty aroma. Throw in a handful of chopped pine nuts. Toss with the pasta and sprouts. Fold through some freshly grated Parmesan cheese and season to taste.

Roasted sprouts with honey and balsamic

Roast quartered sprouts in a medium oven with honey and balsamic vinegar.

Sprout, Swede and Potato Hash

This bears a resemblance to bubble and squeak, but instead of using mashed-up leftovers, the ingredients are kept whole. I think it's perfect as a side dish for braised meat, or as brunch, served with eggs and bacon. You can finish with a few toasted nuts – almonds are particularly good.

Serves 4–6

½ swede, peeled and cut into 2cm chunks
2 tablespoons olive oil
sea salt and freshly ground black pepper
2 potatoes
50g unsalted butter
300g sprouts, trimmed and shredded
1 tablespoon chopped chives or parsley (optional)

Preheat the oven to 200°C/Gas Mark 6.

Toss the swede in half the oil, season and roast in the hot oven for about 20 minutes, until just cooked. Cook the potatoes in boiling salted water for 10 minutes. Drain, peel and cut into 2cm chunks.

In a large, heavy-based frying pan, melt the butter with the rest of the oil. Sauté the potatoes and sprouts together for about 10 minutes, stirring continuously to prevent sticking, and making sure the potatoes are browning and the sprouts wilting. Season well.

Add the swede and continue cooking for 5 minutes until mixed thoroughly. Sprinkle with the herbs (if using) and serve.

Sweet and Sour Red Cabbage

This is based on a dish from Alsace, the far north-eastern corner of France. The cabbage is braised in a mixture of spiced vinegar and wine, but then the dish is sweetened and balanced with sugar and apples. It is great with Duck Confit (see page 45) or any game dish. You can make it ahead of time and reheat.

Serves 4–6

1 small red cabbage
3 onions, sliced
2 apples, quartered, cored and sliced
100g bacon, cut into lardons
2 tablespoons duck fat (you could use butter instead)
2 tablespoons red wine vinegar
375ml red wine
4 juniper berries
2 tablespoons brown sugar
2 tablespoons redcurrant jelly
sea salt and freshly ground black pepper

Cut the cabbage into quarters, remove the core and shred the leaves finely. In a large saucepan, cook the onions, apples and bacon in the duck fat for 3 minutes. When the onions are starting to brown, tip in the cabbage, mix well and cook slowly for 15 minutes. Add the vinegar, wine, juniper berries and sugar. Cover and simmer for about 1½ hours, or until soft.

Remove the cabbage from the liquid with a slotted spoon. Add the redcurrant jelly to the sauce and reduce until the sauce coats the back of a spoon. Remove from the heat and return the cabbage to the pan, mixing with the sauce. Season and serve.

Windy City Salad

This makes a fresh and interesting winter starter. Jerusalem artichokes are great when sliced very thinly and eaten raw, and the flavour works well in combination with finely shredded raw sprouts, goat's cheese and truffle oil. But there can be antisocial side-effects from bringing together root artichokes and sprouts – hence the name! Guy suggests drinking fennel tea.

Serves 4–6

200g Jerusalem artichokes
juice of 1 lemon
1 teaspoon honey
3 tablespoons olive oil
sea salt and freshly ground black pepper
100g winter leaves, washed and dried
200g sprouts, trimmed and very finely shredded
1 tablespoon toasted hazelnuts, chopped
2 tablespoons goat's cheese dressing (see page 114)
drizzle of truffle oil

Peel the Jerusalem artichokes and slice very thinly on a mandolin (you can use a potato peeler instead).

Make a quick dressing with the lemon juice, honey and oil. Season. Toss the artichokes, winter leaves and sprouts all together in a bowl with the dressing.

Arrange on a serving dish, sprinkle with the hazelnuts and drizzle with goat's cheese dressing and truffle oil.

Leek and Blue Cheese Sauce

This rich, wintry sauce is incredibly flexible. At our Christmas celebrations at the Field Kitchen, we often serve it drizzled over slices of freshly grilled polenta, as part of the antipasti. You could also use it to create a simple meal with penne or some potato gnocchi, and it would be equally good over some braised kale.

Makes enough for 6 slices of grilled polenta, or to go with 300g penne or gnocchi

3 large leeks, trimmed, washed and thinly sliced
8 sage leaves, shredded
2 tablespoons extra virgin olive oil
1 garlic clove, crushed
200ml double cream
100g mascarpone
sea salt and freshly ground black pepper
150g blue cheese (preferably Gorgonzola), crumbled
1 tablespoon Parmesan cheese, finely grated
1 tablespoon walnuts, toasted and chopped

In a large heavy-based pan, cook the leeks and sage leaves in the olive oil, without browning, until tender. Cook gently for 15 minutes. Add the garlic and cook for another few minutes, before adding the cream and mascarpone. Season well.

Bring up to a simmer. Remove from the heat and add the blue cheese. Sprinkle with Parmesan and walnuts to serve.

Chestnut and Squash Soup with Bacon and Sage

A thick and warming soup, perfect for a cold day. It makes a great starter to a hearty winter meal, but served with some good bread is filling enough to be a meal in itself. Add a little Parmesan and cream to serve, if you like.

Serves 4

1 onion, finely chopped
1 celery stick, finely chopped
1 carrot, finely chopped
1 leek, finely chopped
2 tablespoons olive oil
150g smoked streaky bacon, finely sliced
2 garlic cloves, finely chopped
2 dried chillies, stalks removed, deseeded if preferred, finely chopped
leaves from 1 small bunch of sage, chopped
200g peeled, vacuum-packed chestnuts
1 pumpkin or squash, peeled and chopped
400ml hot chicken stock
sea salt and freshly ground black pepper

Cook the onion, celery, carrot and leek in the oil for about 15 minutes over a low heat. Add the bacon and cook for 10 minutes more without browning. Add the garlic, chillies and sage and cook for 5 minutes.

Then add the chestnuts, squash and enough chicken stock to cover. Simmer for 20 minutes or until the squash is cooked. Take out a cup of the soup and blend it in a food processor. Return it to the pan, taste and adjust the seasoning.

Potato Pizza

This is based on a recipe from *Italian Cooking* by Susanna Gelmetti and is very simple to make. It is a lovely Pugliese dish, with sunny flavours that will brighten up the dark days of midwinter. I think it's fine to cook it in December, as it works well with tinned tomatoes, so it doesn't matter that fresh aren't at their best. You could, of course, make it with fresh tomatoes in the summer. It's a lovely snack, or simple meal, and you eat it hot or cold.

Serves 4–6

1kg potatoes, scrubbed well or peeled
150ml extra virgin olive oil
1 onion, finely sliced
2 garlic cloves, crushed
10 tomatoes, chopped, or 400g tinned tomatoes, chopped
sea salt and freshly ground black pepper
handful of basil, shredded
100g pitted black olives
4 anchovy fillets, chopped
2 tablespoons capers, rinsed and chopped

Preheat the oven to 200°C/Gas Mark 6.

Boil the potatoes and, when cooked, drain well, then mash roughly with about 4 tablespoons of the olive oil.

Cook the onion in a little oil for about 5 minutes until soft. Add the garlic and tomatoes and simmer for 10 minutes. Season well and add the basil.

Line an oiled oven dish with half the potato mixture. Spread with half the tomato sauce. Sprinkle with the olives, anchovies and capers. Top with the rest of the sauce, finishing with the remaining potatoes.

Drizzle with the rest of the oil and bake for 20 minutes until the top becomes golden.

Baked Sprouts with a Stuffing Crust

Sprout haters may well be converted by this seasonal dish that truly makes the most of sprouts. It wouldn't look out of place alongside chicken or sausages, or even with some roast turkey.

Serves 4–6

750g sprouts
3 tablespoons duck fat or butter
1 teaspoon caster sugar
sea salt and freshly ground black pepper
100g smoked streaky bacon, chopped
1 garlic clove, crushed
1 tablespoon chopped sage leaves
1 teaspoon thyme leaves
150g soft breadcrumbs
finely grated zest of 1 orange
1 tablespoon chopped parsley
100g peeled, vacuum-packed chestnuts, roughly chopped
200ml chicken stock

Preheat the oven to 160°C/Gas Mark 3.

Peel and trim the sprouts and cut into quarters lengthways. Toss in an oven-proof dish with 1 tablespoon of the duck fat and the sugar and season well. Bake in the oven for about 15 minutes, until just tender.

While the sprouts are cooking, brown the bacon in a frying pan in the remaining duck fat, then add the garlic, sage and thyme. Cook for 1 more minute, remove from the heat and stir through the breadcrumbs, orange zest and parsley. Season.

Stir the chestnuts into the sprouts. Pour over the chicken stock. Top with the stuffing mixture and return to the oven for 10 minutes, or until golden.

Roast Parsnips with a Yoghurt and Date Sauce

Russell Goodwin, who worked for several years at the Field Kitchen, came up with this inventive dish. I really like how the sourness of the yoghurt contrasts with the sweet roasted parsnips. You could combine it with a selection of other North African-inspired vegetable dishes to make a complete meal, or serve it as a side dish with the Chermoulah Chicken or stuffed lamb shoulder (see pages 254 and 123).

Serves 4–6

1kg parsnips
30g unsalted butter, melted
1 tablespoon olive oil
sea salt and freshly ground black pepper
1 tablespoon maple syrup
finely grated zest and juice of 1 orange
1 garlic clove, crushed
1 red chilli, deseeded if preferred, finely chopped
juice of 1 lemon
pinch of ground cumin
200ml plain yoghurt
75g pitted dates, finely chopped
1 tablespoon chopped mint (optional)

Preheat the oven to 190°C/Gas Mark 5.

Peel the parsnips and cut into quarters lengthways, cutting out the cores if woody. Toss in the butter and oil. Season well and mix through the maple syrup and orange zest and juice.

Roast in an ovenproof tray for about 40 minutes, until tender. Meanwhile, mix together all the other ingredients except the mint to make the dressing.

To serve, drizzle the roasted parsnips with the yoghurt sauce and sprinkle with the mint (if using).

Potato, Jerusalem Artichoke and Porcini Gratin

It is the incredibly flavoursome porcini mushroom reduction, mixed with cream, that makes this gratin. The flavours combine well with the Jerusalem artichokes to create something special. You can make a slightly different version, using Jerusalem artichokes, leeks and thyme. Simply soften the leeks, add the thyme and cream, and mix with artichokes and potatoes in place of the porcini mixture. But I think this original version is the best.

Serves 6–8

50g dried porcini
1 tablespoon olive oil
3 garlic cloves, crushed
1 teaspoon thyme leaves
200ml double cream
sea salt and freshly ground black pepper
500g potatoes, peeled
500g Jerusalem artichokes, peeled and kept in acidulated water
1 tablespoon finely grated Parmesan cheese

Preheat the oven to 180°C/Gas Mark 4.

Soak the dried porcini in 400ml boiling water for at least 20 minutes. Drain and squeeze out the excess moisture from the mushrooms, reserving the soaking liquor. Finely chop the porcini and cook for 5 minutes in the olive oil. Add the garlic and thyme and cook for another couple of minutes before adding the reserved mushroom soaking liquor. Increase the heat and reduce the mushroom stock until there are only a few tablespoons left. Add the cream, bring to a boil, remove from the heat and season well.

Thinly slice the potatoes and artichokes. Mix together in a bowl and season. Add the mushroom cream and mix well until the vegetables are coated. Tip into an ovenproof dish, cover with foil and bake for 1 hour in the oven. Remove the foil, sprinkle with the Parmesan and return to the oven for 5 minutes until browned on top.

Stuffed Dates with Clementines and Pomegranates

This is an incredibly fresh and pretty dessert that uses seasonal fruit unusually and is a welcome break from all the heavy puddings we tend to eat at this time of year. It's based on a recipe by the brilliant Californian cook Judy Rogers.

Serves 4–6

12 dates
1 tablespoon unsalted pistachios, lightly toasted and chopped
seeds from ½ pomegranate
2 tablespoons mascarpone
finely grated zest of 1 orange and 2 teaspoons orange juice
few drops of orange flower water
8 clementines

Remove the stones from the dates by slitting each one open and removing it, while keeping the date whole.

Mix half the pistachios and pomegranate seeds with the mascarpone and stir in the orange zest and about 2 teaspoons of juice (or to taste) and the orange flower water. Using a teaspoon, carefully stuff each date with a little of the mixture.

Remove the skins and pith from the clementines and cut each fruit across into thin slices. Place on a serving plate. Place the dates on top and finish with the extra pistachios and pomegranate seeds.

Partridge and Cabbage

This is a classic combination of ingredients, and it is all cooked in one pot. Partridges are generally available during the autumn and winter, and our grey-legged (or English) partridge has a delicate, gamey flavour. Take care not to overcook the breasts – they should still be slightly pink inside and firm to the touch, with a little give – but also make sure the legs are cooked through – the meat will be easy to cut through and coming away from the bone.

Serves 4

4 partridges
1 tablespoon olive oil
25g unsalted butter, plus 25g more to finish
sea salt and freshly ground black pepper
200g smoked streaky bacon, cut into lardons
1 carrot, very finely chopped
1 celery stick, very finely chopped
1 leek, very finely chopped
1 red onion, chopped
1 bay leaf
1 sprig of thyme
3 garlic cloves, crushed
125ml white wine
250ml good chicken stock
1 Savoy cabbage, cored and shredded

Preheat the oven to 180°C/Gas Mark 4.

In a flameproof casserole, brown the partridges all over in the oil and butter. Season and remove from the pan.

Add the bacon, carrot, celery, leek and red onion to the pan with the bay and thyme and cook slowly for 10 minutes. Add the garlic and cook for 1 minute, then pour in the wine. Increase the heat and reduce, scraping the pan, until only a few tablespoons of liquid are left. Add the stock, bring to a simmer and return the partridges. Cover and place in the oven for about 15 minutes.

Meanwhile, blanch the cabbage in boiling salted water for 2 minutes. Drain well. Check the partridges are done to your liking, and remove them from the casserole. Quickly carve the legs from the carcasses and return to the pan; leave the breasts on the bone to rest in a warm place. Increase the heat, add the cabbage to the partridge juices and simmer for 5 minutes, until the juices are reduced and the cabbage cooked.

Check the seasoning, remove from the heat and stir in the remaining butter. Serve with the partridge breasts – on or off the bone.

Celeriac and Chestnut Pie

We served this as the vegetarian centrepiece for last year's Field Kitchen Christmas. For meat-eaters, you can add good-quality sausage meat to the filling, a bit more booze and use it as a great stuffing for turkey. The pie should be served with Cumberland sauce.

Serves 6–8

1 tablespoon groundnut oil
1 small onion, chopped
1 celery stick, chopped
½ celeriac, peeled and very finely chopped
1 garlic clove, chopped
175g peeled, vacuum-packed chestnuts
50g walnuts, chopped
50g cashew nuts (or brazils or almonds), chopped
2 eggs
½ teaspoon thyme leaves
½ teaspoon chopped marjoram leaves
1 tablespoon brandy
finely grated zest of ½ orange
sea salt
cayenne pepper
1 x shortcrust pastry (see page 244)
plain flour, to dust
Cumberland sauce, to serve

Heat the oil in a pan and sweat the onion, celery and celeriac for 5–10 minutes, until soft, adding the garlic for the last minute. Remove from the heat and add all the nuts. Mix in one of the eggs, the herbs, brandy, orange zest, salt and cayenne pepper to taste.

Roll out the pastry on a lightly floured surface into a large oblong, 6mm thick. Lift carefully on to a baking sheet and trim to even up the edges. Beat the remaining egg. Pile the filling down the centre of the oblong, then brush the edges of the pastry with beaten egg and bring them together over the filling, to enclose completely. Pinch the edges to seal firmly, as if making a pasty. Trim off any excess and use the trimmings to decorate.

Leave to rest in the fridge for 30 minutes while you preheat the oven to 220°C/Gas Mark 7. Brush the pie with beaten egg and bake in the hot oven for 10 minutes, then reduce the oven temperature to 160°C/Gas Mark 3 and cook for a further 20 minutes.

Serve hot, sliced thickly, with Cumberland sauce.

Cumberland Sauce

Matt Prowse, Mitch Tonk's partner at The Seahorse in Dartmouth, kindly sent me this recipe.

zest of 1 lemon
zest and juice of 1 orange
2 shallots, finely chopped
200ml port
20g redcurrant jelly
1 teaspoon mustard powder
pinch of cayenne
juice of ½ lemon

Cook the lemon and orange zest for 3 minutes in boiling water and then drain well. Simmer the shallots in the port for 10 minutes.

Add the redcurrant to the port and whisk together over a low heat for 5 minutes. Pass through a sieve and discard the shallots.

Return the jelly mixture to the pan and add the mustard, cayenne and zest. Add the orange and lemon juice and mix well.

Mixed Winter Vegetables with Brown Butter and Almonds

We regularly feature this dish on the Christmas menu at the Field Kitchen. Preparing sprouts for a full house of diners is a lot of work and I also think it's nice to have a bit of variation, so we add some other brassicas, use different cooking methods and finish with the brown butter and almonds. As with cauliflower, we find it's often best to roast sprouts rather than boil them – the flavour intensifies, and there's much less chance of them becoming soggy. This dish is also very good with the addition of some steamed leeks.

Serves 4–6

300g sprouts, trimmed and quartered
½ cauliflower, broken into florets
1 tablespoon olive oil
1 teaspoon caster sugar
sea salt and freshly ground black pepper
300g cavolo nero, leaves removed from the stems
50g unsalted butter
1 garlic clove, crushed
1 teaspoon thyme leaves
50g toasted flaked almonds, smashed up

Preheat the oven to 180°C/Gas Mark 4.

Toss the sprout quarters and cauliflower florets together in the oil and sugar and season well. Roast in a baking tray for 20 minutes until browned and tender.

Meanwhile, blanch the kale in boiling salted water for 3 minutes. Drain, refresh in cold water and squeeze out any excess water. Chop roughly and season.

Remove the sprouts and cauliflower from the oven and toss them through the kale. Keep warm.

In a small frying pan, melt the butter. When it's brown, add the garlic and thyme. Immediately pour over the vegetables with the almonds, mix well and season.

Sticky Toffee Pudding

Joyce Molyneux's sticky toffee pudding, originally served when Joyce ran the Carved Angel restaurant in Dartmouth, is probably the best I've ever eaten. The original recipe is a firm favourite at the Field Kitchen and a few years ago we gave it a Christmas twist by adding prunes and tipping in a load of booze. Serve as an alternative to Christmas Pudding.

Makes 2 x 900ml pudding basins/Serves 10–12

200g prunes, chopped
55g dried figs, chopped
1½ teaspoons bicarbonate of soda
85g soft unsalted butter, plus more for the basins
250g caster sugar
a few drops of vanilla extract
2 eggs
350g self-raising flour
1½ teaspoons baking powder
1 tablespoon brandy

For the topping:
350g dark muscovado sugar
200g unsalted butter
150ml double cream

Place the prunes, figs, 425ml boiling water and the bicarbonate of soda in a bowl and set aside to cool.

Put all the topping ingredients in a saucepan and heat for 3 minutes until the sugar has dissolved. Pour into two buttered 900ml pudding basins.

In a large bowl, cream the butter with the caster sugar and vanilla until light and fluffy. Gradually beat in the eggs. Sift the flour and baking powder together and fold in to make a batter, adding the brandy towards the end. Stir the fruit mixture into the batter and divide evenly between the basins.

Cover each basin with foil and tie securely with string, leaving long ends. Knot the ends to make a handle across the basin so it can be easily lifted into the steamer.

Place the basins on trivets in two large pans and pour in enough hot water to come halfway up the sides. Cover and steam for 1½ hours. Check every 20 minutes or so that the pan has not boiled dry and keep topping up with boiling water. Lift out of the water and turn the puddings out on to a warmed serving dish. Serve immediately.

Introducing the Riverford Cooks

Our Riverford Cooks help us out with recipe ideas and events and some have kindly contributed to this book. Here is a little more information about them, along with an introduction to a couple of our very first Cooks. Many more are based countrywide, inspiring others to cook seasonally.

Anna Colquhoun

Anna trained in San Francisco and did a stint at Chez Panisse (Guy's inspiration for the Riverford Field Kitchen). Anna now teaches fun hands-on cooking classes in London. Her recent book, *Eat Slow Britain*, was published as part of the Alastair Sawday collection. www.culinaryanthropologist.org

Cooking tip: After boiling your broad beans, refresh them in cold water and slip them out of their bitter, rubbery skins. It sounds like a faff, but is worth it for the beans' hugely improved flavour, colour and texture.

Francesca Melman

Francesca has spent over 15 years working as a chef in some of London's top restaurants, including The River Café, Alistair Little's and Baker and Spice, as well as stages at Chez Panisse and Rick Stein's Seafood Restaurant. Currently she runs her own catering business providing private dinner and lunch parties. francescamelman@hotmail.com

Cooking tip: To keep as much flavour as possible when blanching spinach, cavolo nero or chard, don't refresh under cold water. Instead lay out over a large surface area such as a tea towel to cool down quickly. This can then be used to squeeze out excess water when necessary.

Mark Bader

Based in Brighton, Mark is a travel and food photographer as well as a cook, his work taking him to some exotic locations. He has a relaxed and fun approach to cooking and originally started working with Riverford as an enthusiastic amateur cook. shopcookandeat.blogspot.com

Cooking tip: Roast beetroot on a bed of sea salt, covered with foil. This draws out the excess liquid, and works perfectly when roasting with butter and balsamic vinegar or for soups.

Sylvain Jamois

From a young age, Sylvain was inspired to cook by his grandmother, who owned a traditional bistro in France. In London, Sylvain has worked at Moro, Neal's Yard and Green and Black's, among others. He now heads up his own catering company and was one of our very first Riverford Cooks. He regularly cooks at farm events for us and makes a mean garlic soup. undercoverkitchen. gmail.com

Cooking tip: Onions release volatile gases that, when in contact with the water on our eyeballs, turn into a mild form of acid that makes us cry. You can suppress this by keeping your onions in the fridge for about an hour before chopping them. Don't forget to put some bread in your ears, a spoon in your mouth, a banana in your back pocket and whatever else the old wives tell you to do!

Lisa Silcock

Lisa launched her business, Black Pot Catering, following a career in TV documentaries. She caters for events and parties of all sizes, using predominantly seasonal and organic produce. Lisa has helped us with the recipes we send out in our veg boxes each week and publish online. www.blackpot.co.uk

Cooking tip: For a fantastic easy garnish, finely dice some red onion, put in a small bowl and cover in red or white wine vinegar. Leave for an hour or so, then drain off the vinegar. The red onion will have turned a brilliant bright pink and will be mellow yet tangy tasting. Sprinkle over salads, dips, fish dishes.

Index

Index

Index